TURN YOUR BACKYARD INTO THE ultimate BBQ hotspot with Anthony Anderson and Cedric The Entertainer, comedic royalty and hosts of A&E's *Kings of BBQ*. In their hometowns of Compton and St. Louis, Anthony and Cedric saw BBQ as more than just food—it was a love language that brought family and friends together with grill smoke, ribs falling off the bone, and dancing.

AC Barbeque takes you on a mouthwatering cross-country tour to capture the soul of BBQ in St. Louis, Memphis, the Carolinas, and elsewhere. You'll find sizzling recipes ranging from pork belly burnt ends to dry rub beef brisket to jerk ribs, plus other favorites like macaroni salad, baked beans, fried catfish, and hush puppies. There are even snacks and desserts like fried pickles and peach cobbler, and, maybe best of all, a whole chapter on sauces and rubs.

Whether you're a seasoned pitmaster or firing up your backyard grill for the first time, this book is a celebration of the rich traditions, bold flavors, and undeniable joy of barbequing. So dust off your tongs, grab your apron, and join Anthony and Cedric for a smokin' hot adventure.

BARBEQUE

BARBEQUE

THE HUSKY AND HANDSOME GUIDE TO GRILLING

FROM THE KINGS OF BBQ
ANTHONY ANDERSON AND
CEDRIC THE ENTERTAINER

with Garrett McGrath

SIMON ELEMENT
NEW YORK AMSTERDAM/ANTWERP LONDON
TORONTO SYDNEY/MELBOURNE NEW DELHI

RED ROOSTER
LOUISIANA
HOT
SAUCE

For those who cook the food before they yell to come and eat.

Anthony: For my father.

Cedric: To my uncle Lloyd.

OUR SMOKIN' HOT CONTENTS

TEXAS TWIST
Four Styles Collide for BBQ Bliss

OTHER AMERICAN FAVORITES

SNACKS, DESSERTS & DRINKS

THE PANTRY

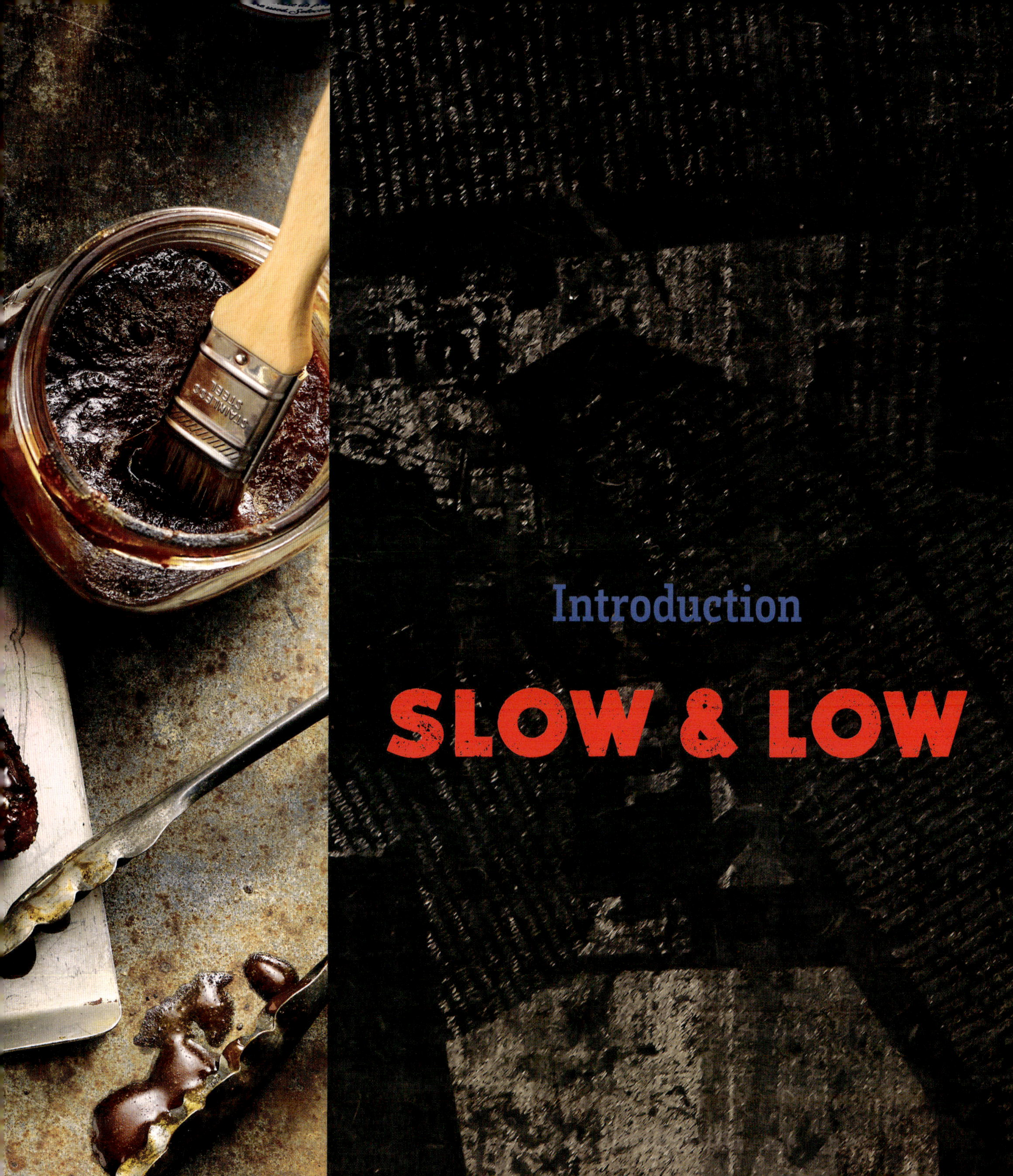

Introduction

SLOW & LOW

GET LOST IN THE SAUCE WITH AC BARBEQUE'S SMOKIN' HOT BOOK!

Y'ALL EVER CRAVE THAT BACKYARD COOKOUT MAGIC? The kind where the air's thick with smoke, the ribs are fallin' off the bone, and the music's got everyone shakin' a leg? That's AC Barbeque, baby! And we ain't just talkin' about delicious grub, we're talkin' about family, community, and keepin' the flame of Black BBQ burnin' bright.

When we were growing up in Compton and St. Louis, BBQ was more than just food—it was a love language. So when we started AC Barbeque and our show, we knew we had to shine a light on the stories, the recipes, and the soul that goes into every smoky bite. It's about the family-run joints passed down through generations, the pitmasters who weave magic with fire and spice, and the folks who come together to celebrate good food and good times.

Now we're takin' it one step further with our smokin' hot book! Get ready for a cross-country tour of the savoriest, smokehouse-filled corners of the BBQ universe. We'll introduce you to the kings and queens who inspired us, the musicians who keep the Grill & Chill vibes flowin', and, of course, the AC fam who's been rockin' with us since day one.

This ain't just a recipe book, though. It's the ultimate guide to the AC Barbeque lifestyle—the secrets to our fire, the party-pumpin' tunes, and everything it takes to be a true King of BBQ. We're talkin' tips, tricks, and enough stories to fill your belly and your soul.

So grab a plate, pull up a chair, and get ready to "get lost in the sauce" with *AC Barbeque.* We'll see you on the road, fam!

—Anthony Anderson and Cedric The Entertainer

P.S.: Don't forget to bring your appetite and your dancin' shoes—things are about to get a whole lotta hot damn!

YOU'RE INVITED
LOVE
HATE

TO THE COOKOUT

BAR 5015
ac
Backyard
Barbeque Party
HOSTED BY
GRILL MASTERS AND FOUNDERS OF AC BARBEQUE
ANTHONY
ANDERSON
+
CEDRIC
THE ENTERTAINER
AC BBQ SAMPLES FROM 6-9P WITH CELEBRITY PIT MASTER JOEY VICTORIAN
FROM NETFLIX BBQ SHOWDOWN SEASON 2
LATE NIGHT BITES F/ AC BARBECUE SAUCES AND SPICES FROM 9P-MID
BACKYARD BBQ GAMES (DOMINOS, SPADES, JENGA)
LIVE DJ AND GREAT VIBES
SUNDAY
BAR 5015
JUNE 23
ac
HOSTED BY
GRILL MASTERS AND FOUNDERS OF
ANTHONY
ANDERSON
+
CEDRIC
FROM NETFLIX BBQ SHOWDOWN SEASON 2
LIVE DJ AND GREAT VIBES
SUNDAY
BAR 5015

STOP

MASTER-TOUCH

AC BARBEQUE'S GUIDE TO THE BEST COOKOUT

Welcome to the AC Barbeque universe, where the grill is hot, the vibes are cool, and the flavors are a whole lotta hot damn! Ready to turn your backyard into the ultimate BBQ kingdom? Let's get started.

RULE 1

FAMILY FIRST, BBQ SECOND

At AC Barbeque, we believe BBQ is more than just food: it's a family affair. So, when you're firing up that grill, remember to invite your AC fam and make it a celebration. After all, you aren't just hosting a BBQ.

RULE 2

SPICE IT UP—DON'T SKIMP ON THE SMOKE

Don't bite your fingers trying to resist the urge—get that grill goin' and don't skimp on the smoke! Our recipes are designed to elevate your BBQ game and keep your taste buds doing a two-step with every bite.

RULE 3

HAVE FUN, BUT KEEP IT FUNCTIONAL

AC Barbeque is always a party, but we also value functionality. This cookbook was designed with cooks in mind, solving problems before they start to give you the best results possible. So, whether you're grilling, chilling, or turning up the heat, rest assured that AC Barbeque has got your back.

RULE 4

BRING THE FINESSE, HUSKY AND HANDSOME STYLE

We're not just about BBQ: we're a lifestyle brand. When you step up to the grill with AC Barbeque, you're not just cooking—you're making a statement. So, don't just grill: grill with style. After all, you're husky and handsome, and your BBQ should be too.

RULE 5

BEST FRIENDS IN YOUR MOUTH, LITERALLY

At the end of the day, AC Barbeque is about sharing joy and creating connections. When you eat AC Barbeque, you're not just enjoying a meal; you're sharing a piece of Anthony, Cedric, and the entire AC fam. So, don't be shy. Get lost in the sauce and let the good times roll.

So, there you have it—the AC Barbeque Guide to the Ultimate Cookout. Now grab your tongs, fire up the grill, and let's make some memories! Grill and chill, turn up the heat, and remember—when it comes to BBQ, AC Barbeque is the boss.

LET'S GET COOKIN'!

BARBEQUE

WEST COAST SMOKEOUT

Los Angeles's Cross-Cultural BBQ Feast

FIRE UP YOUR GRILL AND GET READY TO HOLLER "HALLELUJAH!" because we're taking you on a mouthwatering journey through the City of Angels. That's right, Los Angeles, the undisputed champion of diverse eats, boasts a BBQ scene as vibrant and eclectic as its neighborhoods.

Forget the stereotypes of smoky pits and one-note flavors. Here, in this land of sunshine and creativity, BBQ is a beautiful tapestry woven from the rich cultural threads of Asian American traditions, Chicano influences, and the time-tested techniques of Texas smokehouses that went a little farther west. From award-winning legends to innovative pop-ups, LA's BBQ scene has something to satisfy every craving.

We, the AC Barbeque crew, have been on a personal odyssey of exploration, tasting our way through the city's smoky havens. We've shared ribs with James Beard Award–winning chefs, learned the secrets from up-and-coming pitmasters, and even gotten our hands dirty cooking alongside these amazing folks. Now it's your turn to experience the magic!

This LA city guide is your passport to a world of unforgettable BBQ experiences. We'll take you on a tour of our favorite spots—places that embody the true AC spirit: cookin' with passion, fostering a sense of community, and bringing people together over plates piled high with deliciousness. So grab your forks, because it's about to get real good!

THE SPOTS

BLUDSO'S BBQ

It all started in 2008 when Kevin Bludso opened a small walk-up stand in the heart of Compton. But that was only the beginning for Bludso's BBQ, as it's gone on to become a staple in the LA BBQ community. Kevin has brought the fire to the reality scene as a recurring judge on the hit Netflix BBQ competition show *Barbecue Showdown*. We were honored to have him mentor us on *Kings of BBQ*. His James Beard Award–winning cookbook, *Bludso's BBQ Cookbook*, is available now from Ten Speed Press.

WOODY'S BAR-B-QUE

Simply said, Woody's Bar-B-Que is the real deal. Since they opened their doors in 1975, they have catered directly to their community—cooking their meat fresh daily, going from the pit to the steam tables and out the door to the customers. They have since expanded to four locations and have continued cookin' up the same quality meats that made them famous.

BOOTSY'S BBQ

Founded by Armond Keys, Bootsy's BBQ is the true hidden gem of the LA BBQ scene. In the View Park–Windsor Hills neighborhood, you'll smell Bootsy's before you see it, but if you follow your nose, you'll hear a speaker playing some classic R&B and find yourself at a smoker off the back of Armond's International Scout. With his hometown pop-up, Armond is as authentic as it gets: Locals know him for his expert technique and tender meats, from beef ribs, baby backs, and brisket to his mouthwatering salmon.

THE PARK'S FINEST BBQ

The name says it all: The Park's Finest is some of the finest BBQ on the west coast. It all started with founder Johneric Concordia, who created a local catering company in 2009 with a dream of curating the BBQ flavors he grew up with. By 2012, The Park's Finest gained its first sit-down eatery experience in Echo Park, in Historic Filipinotown, all the while still catering parties, weddings, and other events across Southern California. With a fusion of American BBQ and traditional Filipino cuisine, The Park's Finest created a culinary experience of celebration, a product of a group of friends' adventures growing up and cooking on the block. Check out Mama Leah's Coconut Beef as a reflection of the Philippine islands, Ann's Cornbread Bibingka as the experience of growing up in LA, and Big Tony's hood-famous sauce as the soundtrack to it all—mixin' cane, pineapple, simmered soy sauce, peppers, and spices.

ZEF BBQ

Zef BBQ is chef Logan Sandoval's manifesto to his culinary experience: the culture, the cookin', and, most importantly, the people. Amid the pandemic, he and his wife, Anna Lindsey, found themselves at a crossroads, heading back to Logan's hometown of Simi Valley and starting a true family-run BBQ operation out of their garage. An overnight pop-up sensation, Zef BBQ was born just like that. And since then it has spread like wildfire, creating some of the most innovative flavors in the BBQ game. Every weekend, they sell out their rotating menu in minutes. This reputation brought Logan right to the center stage, where he competed and became the runner-up on Netflix's *Barbecue Showdown* season 2.

AC BARBEQUE

AC Barbeque in Century City is our tribute to the pitmasters and backyard legends who taught us what real BBQ is all about. Every rib, brisket, and sausage we smoke is a nod to family, tradition, and the joy of gathering around good food. We built our first location to honor where we come from, to share the flavors we love, and to keep that fire and those stories burning.

COOKING TIME: 6 HOURS

SERVES 4

AIN'T YO ANCHO CHILE BABY BACK RIBS

These Ain't Yo Ancho Chile Baby Back Ribs are a simmering symphony of sweet and spicy! Pork takes center stage, rubbed with a smoky paprika blend and slow-smoked over hickory wood for that fall-off-the-bone tenderness you crave. Then, we hit those ribs with our epic Ancho Chile BBQ Sauce for a bold kick that'll leave you beggin' for more.

¼ cup packed dark brown sugar

¼ cup smoked paprika

¼ cup kosher salt

2 tablespoons garlic powder

1 tablespoon freshly ground black pepper

1 tablespoon onion powder

2 (3-pound) slabs spare ribs, St. Louis–cut, membranes removed

Spray bottle filled with apple cider vinegar

Ancho Chile BBQ Sauce (page 207)

In a bowl, mix up all that kickin' dry rub. We're talkin' brown sugar, paprika, salt, garlic powder, pepper, and onion powder. Get your fingers in there and break up any lumps—gotta make sure those ribs are evenly coated! Now, season the ribs on both sides with this glorious rub. Don't be shy—pile it on!

Smoke show time: Crank up the heat to 225°F in your smoker. Place those seasoned ribs on the rack and close the lid. We're talkin' at least 4½ hours of smoky goodness here. But don't forget to spritz those ribs with some vinegar every hour or so. We gotta keep 'em moist!

After 4½ hours, take the ribs out and brush them with our epic Ancho Chile BBQ Sauce. This sauce is gonna take your ribs to the next level!

Cook for another hour, or until those ribs reach an internal temp of 200°F to 205°F. We're talkin' fall-off-the-bone tender perfection! Take them off the grill and let them rest for 20 minutes at room temperature. Now it's time to chow down! Get ready for compliments and requests for seconds, 'cause these ribs are the real deal.

COOKING TIME:
5 HOURS
(9 HOURS TOTAL TIME)

SERVES 6

SANTA MARIA GRILLED TRI-TIP BEEF

Alright, AC Fam, listen up! Today's recipe is gonna have your taste buds doin' the two-step like they're at a family reunion. We're talkin' Santa Maria Tri-Tip Beef, a legendary BBQ dish that'll turn you into a grillin' champion faster than you can say "Husky and Handsome" (which, by the way, is totally you after you cook this bad boy up).

This tri-tip comes from the bottom sirloin, and when we cook it right (which, trust us, we will), it's gonna be juicy and flavorful and leave you wonderin' why you ever settled for hot dogs.

1 (2½-pound) beef tri-tip roast

Put Me on Everything Rub (page 203)

Kosher salt

⅓ cup red wine vinegar

⅓ cup vegetable oil, plus more for oiling the grill

4 garlic cloves, crushed

½ teaspoon Dijon mustard

First, take your tri-tip roast and coat it in that Put Me on Everything Rub and kosher salt like you're giving it a hug. Make sure it gets everywhere! Then, throw it in a glass baking dish, cover it with plastic wrap, and send it to chill in the fridge for 4 hours. Patience is a virtue, especially when it comes to juicy meat.

While your tri-tip chills, let's make that marinade sing! In a sealable container, combine the vinegar, oil, garlic, and mustard. Shake it well to get everything nice and blended.

Take your tri-tip out of the fridge and let it sit at room temperature for 30 minutes. We want it happy and relaxed before it hits the heat.

Alright, time to break out the grill! Whether you're using a gas fire or building your own fire doesn't matter; get it nice and hot, like you're preheating the party. Don't forget to lightly oil those grates to prevent any stickage disasters.

Now, slap that tri-tip on the grill and brush it with some of that marinade you made earlier. We're talking about every 4 minutes here, flippin' and bastin' like a pro. You want it to cook for 25 to 30 minutes

recipe continues

total, until it's nice and firm with a beautiful reddish-pink center. To be sure, stick an instant-read thermometer in there and make sure it reads 130°F.

Once it's cooked to perfection, let that tri-tip rest for at least 10 minutes before you slice it. This lets all the juices redistribute and makes it even more finger-lickin' good.

There you have it—Santa Maria Tri-Tip that'll have your neighbors beggin' for a bite (but don't share unless they brought a side dish; that's just good BBQ etiquette). Now go forth, grill like a king, and don't forget to wipe that flavor off your face.

COOKING TIME: 7½ HOURS

SERVES 12

LEMON STEPPER PORK BUTT

Y'all ever dream of a meat so juicy, so tender, it'll make you wanna do the two-step with every bite? Well, hold on to your hats, because Lemon Stepper Pork Butt is about to blow your taste buds to kingdom come! This is a slow-cooked symphony of smoky, sweet, and citrusy goodness that'll have you singin' "best friends in your mouth" from the first forkful to the last. To get your hands on our delicious rub, visit our website and order.

1 (4-pound, Husky and Handsome–sized) boneless pork butt

2 tablespoons Dijon mustard

AC Barbeque's Lemon Stepper Rub

Juice of 2 lemons

½ cup Worcestershire sauce

One (12-ounce) can of your favorite light beer

Dr. Cedric's BBQ Sauce (page 202)

First score that pork like a pitmaster: Grab your knife and make crisscross grooves in the fat cap of your pork butt. This ain't just for decoration—it helps that rub penetrate and makes the bark extra crispy (think cracklin' good!).

Cover that pork in a thin layer of mustard to act as your binder. Do not use a thick coat. Next, cover that bad boy in a generous layer of Lemon Stepper Rub. Don't be shy—get in there and massage it in like you're givin' a back rub to your favorite grill partner.

Set your smoker at 275°F and set up your water pan. Once the grill is up to temperature, we're going to let the smoke do its thing. Put your pork butt on the smoker and let it start to get blessed by the fire. How long this takes depends on your smoker, but figure anywhere from 4 to 6 hours, until the internal temperature hits 180°F and the bark sets and looks like a deep mahogany suntan.

When the butt reaches an internal temperature of about 180°F, lay that smoky pork butt in aluminum foil like a cozy blanket. Add some more love in the form of lemon juice, Worcestershire sauce, and a splash of beer (don't worry, the pork won't get drunk; it'll just get even more delicious). Now you have an extra beer you can sip on while the meat finishes. Wrap it up nice and make sure the liquid isn't leaking out.

recipe continues

NOTE: There is no substitute for our Lemon Stepper Rub—it's life changing. But if you need a substitute, please use a tablespoon or two of your favorite lemon pepper spice mixed into ½ cup of Put Me on Everything Rub (page 203).

Back on the smoker it goes, covered in its foil cocoon. Let it simmer in that steamy bath until it's so tender a skewer slides in like butter. This will happen when it hits an internal temp of 205°F, but trust your gut (and your thermometer).

Take that pork butt off the heat and let it rest for at least an hour in a cooler. This lets the juices redistribute and makes shredding a breeze.

Grab your forks or two meat claws and go to town! Pull that pork apart like it's nobody's business. Pile it high on buns, stuff it in tacos, or just eat it by the forkful—it's all good! Serve with our Dr. Cedric's BBQ Sauce.

COOKING TIME:
4½ HOURS
(5 HOURS TOTAL TIME)

SERVES 4

CARNE ASADA PORK BELLY BURNT ENDS

We're turnin' up the heat with some Carne Asada Pork Belly Burnt Ends. This ain't yo grandma's recipe, this is AC Barbeque style, where the only thing sweeter than the glaze is the victory dance you'll be doin' after every bite.

3 pounds skinless pork belly

Carne Asada Dry Rub (page 210)

Spray bottle filled with apple cider vinegar

1 cup Smoky Beer BBQ Sauce (page 205)

First, we're going to dice that bad-boy skinless pork belly into 1-inch cubes. Nice and bite-size for maximum flavor. Coat those pork belly cubes with the Carne Asada Dry Rub like there's no tomorrow. Get it on all sides—don't be shy! Let that flavor sit for at least 30 minutes or go all out and let it marinate in the fridge overnight. We ain't judging, just cookin' up some magic.

When you are ready, get your smoker up to 250°F. We recommend oak, hickory, pecan, or a fruit wood for that extra somethin' somethin'.

Let's smoke it like a boss: Place those seasoned cubes on a sheet pan, fat side down. This is where the magic happens. Throw that pan in the smoker and let the smoke do its thang. Keep an eye on those cubes, though. If they're lookin' a little dry, spritz 'em with some vinegar—a little moisture goes a long way.

Smoke those cubes until they're feelin' nice and tender. We're talkin' around 195°F internal temp, which took us about 3 hours. Patience is a virtue, especially when it comes to burnt ends.

Let's get to that burnt-end bliss. Grab an aluminum pan and dump those smoky pork belly cubes in there. Time to get saucy! Toss the cubes in that glorious Smoky Beer BBQ Sauce until they're lookin' good enough to eat (but don't eat 'em yet!).

Throw that uncovered pan back in the smoker and let the caramelization work its magic. We're talkin' 45 minutes of pure, sticky goodness.

After they've caramelized, let those burnt ends cool for a sec (trust us, you don't wanna burn your mouth on pure deliciousness), then DIG IN!

Cali Love Slaw, p. 39

Ain't Yo Ancho Chile Baby Back Ribs, p. 22

COOKING TIME:
3½ HOURS
(6½ HOURS TOTAL TIME)

SERVES 4

CHICKEN AND WAFFLES

We're talkin' breakfast royalty right here! Chicken and Waffles didn't originate in Los Angeles, but it's become a staple of La La Land. This is a flavor explosion that combines golden-fried chicken so good you'll wanna shout with light and fluffy waffles begging for a drizzle of some real maple syrup.

1 cup whole buttermilk

2 tablespoons hot sauce

8 tablespoons Old Vienna Red Hot Riplets Seasoning, divided (see Note)

4 boneless, skinless chicken thighs

1½ cups all-purpose flour

1 teaspoon freshly ground black pepper

Vegetable oil

1 box of your favorite waffle mix, prepared per package instructions

Real maple syrup

Softened salted butter

Combine that buttermilk, hot sauce, and 4 tablespoons of your Red Hot Riplets Seasoning in a zip-top bag. Throw in those chicken thighs, seal it up tight, and let it marinate in the fridge for at least 3 hours or overnight for maximum flavor.

In a shallow dish, combine your flour, remaining Red Hot Riplets Seasoning, and pepper. Take that marinated chicken out, one piece at a time, and coat it well in that dredge mixture. Press it in there to make sure it sticks, then shake off any excess.

Heat some 3 inches of vegetable oil in a big ol' Dutch oven to 350°F. Carefully add a few pieces of that dredged chicken and fry them until they're golden brown and cooked through, about 10 minutes. Once they're golden and crispy, take them out and let them drain on paper towels—gotta get rid of that excess oil!

Now it's time to plate up this masterpiece! Stack those waffles on a plate, top them with your crispy, juicy chicken, and then drizzle everything with real maple syrup and a pat of that softened butter. This Chicken and Waffles combo is the ultimate breakfast (or brunch, or lunch, or dinner) champion, and it's guaranteed to leave you feelin' satisfied like royalty.

NOTE: **If you can't get Old Vienna Red Hot Riplets Seasoning from your grocery store or the internet, you can use your favorite hot or Cajun seasoning instead.**

COOKING TIME:
25 MINUTES

SERVES 6

CHILI MAC AND CHEESE

Craving a hearty, cheesy, chili-licious meal that's ready in 25 minutes flat? Look no further than AC's Chili Mac and Cheese! This has an energetic tang that combines juicy ground beef, fire-roasted tomatoes, and creamy melted cheese with a kickin' chili spice blend. All in one pot, for easy cookin' and minimal cleanup!

1 tablespoon olive oil

1 onion, finely chopped

2 garlic cloves, minced

1 red bell pepper, seeded and chopped

3 tablespoons Carne Asada Dry Rub (page 210)

1 pound ground beef (90/10 is ideal)

1 (28-ounce) can crushed canned tomatoes

1 (15-ounce) can red kidney beans, rinsed and drained

2½ cups beef broth

2 cups elbow macaroni pasta

8 ounces shredded Monterey Jack cheese

Kosher salt

Freshly ground black pepper

¼ cup finely chopped fresh cilantro leaves

Fire up your stove on high heat and add that olive oil to a large pot. Throw in the onion and garlic and cook it, stirring, for a minute. Add the bell pepper and keep cookin', stirring, until that onion is nice and translucent, 4 to 5 more minutes.

Add the Carne Asada Dry Rub and stir to combine. Now it's time for the beef! Add it to the pot and crumble it up as you go. Keep cookin', stirring occasionally, until that beef turns from red to a beautiful brown, about 5 minutes.

Once your beef is browned to perfection, add the tomatoes, beans, broth, and macaroni. Give it a good stir. Cover the pot and let it simmer until the macaroni is al dente, about 12 minutes. You want it to be saucy, but not soupy.

Turn off the heat but keep that pot right where it is. Stir in half of that cheese until it's nice and melty. Taste and adjust the salt and pepper to your likin'. Top it all off with the remaining cheese, put the lid back on, and let it sit for 2 minutes. That cheese will be melty and gooey in no time! Grab a plate and pile on that cheesy chili mac goodness. Sprinkle with some cilantro for a pop of color and dig in!

COOKING TIME: 1 HOUR

SERVES 6

CALI LOVE SLAW

Ditch the boring, basic cabbage and get ready for some charred, smoky goodness with this Cali Love Slaw. Forget about fussy prep work like shredding or oiling. We're talkin' whole cabbages thrown straight over the fire for a slow and smoky roast. Blackened exteriors give way to a surprisingly tender interior, infused with that irresistible campfire flavor.

1 cup sour cream
1 cup chopped fresh cilantro leaves
1 tablespoon lime juice
1 tablespoon canned chipotle en adobo, minced (optional)
Kosher salt
Freshly ground black pepper
1 small purple cabbage
1 small green cabbage

First, we're going to whip up that dressing. You can make this the night before if you are short on time. It's like a flavor explosion waiting to happen. Just whisk together the sour cream, cilantro, lime juice, chipotle en adobo (if you're usin' it), a pinch of salt, and a pinch of pepper in a bowl. Cover the bowl and store in your refrigerator.

Get your grill fired up and ready to go. You want some good heat, but leave about a third of the grill free of coals for a cool zone. If you're using gas, crank one burner to high. Once the fire's ready, toss those whole cabbages right on there!

Let the cabbages roast over the open flames, turnin' them every few minutes and lettin' them hang out on the cooler side of the grill every now and then. We want them charred, blistered, and a little soft. This should take 30 to 45 minutes. Don't worry—we're not trying to burn them to a crisp, just cookin' them aggressively. Most of that blackened exterior will get tossed later.

Once the cabbages are nice and blackened and softened up (you should be able to easily slide a knife in there), take them off the heat and let them cool a bit. Then, peel off most of those blackened outer leaves. Cut each cabbage in half, remove the cores, and slice them up thin, just like you would for coleslaw. Add all those beautiful, smoky cabbage ribbons to a big bowl.

Pour about ½ cup of that dressing over the cabbage and toss it to coat everything evenly. Keep adding dressing until all the cabbage is coated and lookin' good. Give it a taste and adjust the seasonings if needed.

Serve this up with your favorite grilled meats or enjoy it all on its own!

COOKING TIME:
50 MINUTES

SERVES 6

KOREAN HOT CAULIFLOWER WINGS

Calling all spice lovers and plant-based foodies—gather 'round! These Korean Hot Cauliflower Wings are about to become your new favorite snack or appetizer.

We're talkin' tender cauliflower florets dipped in a crispy, flavorful batter, then tossed in a sweet and spicy gochujang sauce. Served with a creamy mayo dip for coolin' things down (or not, if you're wantin' to feel the heat), this recipe has the bold kick you're looking for.

1 medium head of cauliflower

¾ cup all-purpose flour

1 cup milk

2 teaspoons garlic powder, divided

Kosher salt

Freshly ground black pepper

¼ cup gochujang (Korean red chile paste), plus 1 teaspoon for dip

¼ cup soy sauce

2½ tablespoons agave syrup

1½ tablespoons rice vinegar

1 tablespoon toasted sesame oil

Juice of ½ lime

½ teaspoon ground ginger

½ cup mayonnaise

2 scallions, finely chopped

Crank your oven to 350°F—it's gonna get hot in here! Grab that cauliflower and chop it up into bite-size florets. It should make at least 25 pieces. Line two baking sheets with parchment paper—gotta keep things clean!

In a bowl, whisk together the flour, milk, 1 teaspoon of garlic powder, a pinch of salt, and a pinch of pepper until you have a smooth, pancake-batter consistency. Not too runny, not too thick.

Using a fork, dunk those cauliflower florets into the batter, making sure they get a nice, even coat. Let any excess batter drip off before placing them on the baking sheet. Pop those florets in the oven and set the timer for 10 minutes. After 10 minutes, use a spatula to carefully flip them over and bake for another 10 minutes.

While the cauliflower bakes, whip up that amazing gochujang marinade! Just mix your ¼ cup of gochujang, soy sauce, agave syrup, rice vinegar, toasted sesame oil, lime juice, ginger, and the remaining teaspoon of garlic powder in a bowl.

After 20 minutes of baking time, take out those florets and brush them generously with that gochujang sauce. Pop the glazed florets back in the oven for another 5 to 10 minutes or until they're nice and crispy. Feel free to give them an extra layer of sauce if you have some left over!

In another bowl, we're going to make the mayo dipper. Stir up the mayo, the remaining teaspoon of gochujang, and a pinch of pepper.

Serve those hot and crispy gochujang cauliflower wings with a side of the mayo dip. Garnish with scallions for a pop of color and freshness.

ST. LOUIS STYLES

Fast, Sweet & Vinegar Bliss

ALRIGHT, GATHER 'ROUND AND LISTEN UP! There's no Cedric The Entertainer without St. Louis. That's right, the Lou is where it all began—the laughter, the love of community, and, of course, the legendary St. Louis BBQ. This city's got a special kind of magic, and it all starts with smokin'-good eats.

So buckle up, 'cause we're taking you on a mouthwatering journey through St. Louis with a true local legend—yours truly, Cedric The Entertainer! This AC Barbeque STL City Guide is your personal VIP pass to the best BBQ spots in town.

We'll be hittin' all the highlights, from the old-school joints that have been smokin' ribs since forever to the innovative new spots that are putting their own unique spin on classic St. Louis flavors. We're talkin' tangy, sweet, and smoky goodness that'll have your taste buds singin' the blues (in the best way possible).

But it ain't just about the food. St. Louis is all about community, and some of my favorite memories are tied to these legendary BBQ spots. We'll be cruisin' past the Fox Theatre, where dreams are made and laughter fills the air. And, of course, we gotta make a pit stop at my star on the St. Louis Walk of Fame—a reminder that anything is possible with a little hard work and a whole lot of BBQ.

So, are you ready to experience St. Louis like a true local? Let's get goin'! This city guide will take you on a delicious adventure that's more than just food—it's a celebration of St. Louis's vibrant spirit, rich history, and smokin'-good BBQ! Get ready to eat like a king (or queen), laugh like you mean it, and feel the warmth of St. Louis hospitality. It's gonna be legendary!

THE SPOTS

C&K

In St. Louis, sauce is boss, and C&K is king. Cedric's hometown favorite was founded by Forris King in 1963, and the BBQ spot has been regarded as an STL classic ever since. C&K's unique spin on BBQ involves new takes on old flavors, from their delicious smoked meats to their house-made sweet and tangy sauce and savory potato salad. The restaurant still keeps it old-school in true St. Louis fashion, preparing the whole pig—or, as they say in STL, "from the rooter to the tooter." It's a must-do for the Lou!

GRILL HOUSE SMOKE HOUSE

Grill House Smoke House is the new kid on the block, but that hasn't stopped owner Jasmine Gaines from bringing lots of love and vibrant flavor to the community. A local favorite, the smoked turkey tips are lathered in that classic St. Louis BBQ sauce that makes everything taste irresistible. And if you're not sure what you want, Grill House has got you covered with their try-before-you-buy policy and generous samples. It's a classic in the making!

RED'S THE ONE AND ONLY BBQ

It's in the name: There's no BBQ like Red's the One and Only! "Blessed to Be the Best," Red's is known for potato salad, ribs, and, of course, that classic sweet potato pie. The welcoming atmosphere and staff make every trip to Red's feel like home. Check 'em out for delicious food and good vibes—just be sure not to bite your fingers!

PAPPY'S SMOKEHOUSE

Pappy's Smokehouse is all about simplicity and creating the best BBQ experience possible for the whole fam. To this day, Pappy's continues this spirit at their two locations in Midtown St. Louis and St. Peters, Missouri. It's all about cookin' and community around these parts!

KENRICK'S MEATS

Everyone in the STL knows Kenrick's Meats. It's timeless, delicious, and reliable. But many of them don't know that it all started in the humble back of a refrigerator truck. In 1945, founder Herb Kenrick grew his business by using his truck to deliver fresh meats to the people of St. Louis. In just a few years, Herb's business was the talk of the town, leading him to a permanent location and sale to Joe Weinmann, aka "Joe the Butcher," who we met on our trip to the Lou. Joe and his butchers are true masters of meat, innovative and creative with their specialty meats, like the Ozark Grillers, bacon-wrapped seasoned beef with cheddar cheese. Always staying true to their history and values, Kenrick's continues to use Herb's recipes for their OG sausages and famous landjaeger—a dried, cured smoked sausage.

COOKING TIME:
3 HOURS
(27 HOURS TOTAL TIME)

SERVES 6

ST. LOUIS–STYLE RIBS

Calling all grill masters and BBQ enthusiasts! Get ready to raise the roof with these St. Louis–style ribs. We're talkin' soulful Southern flavor, fall-off-the-bone tenderness, and enough juicy goodness to make your taste buds sing.

2 (2- to 3-pound) St. Louis–style pork rib slabs, membranes removed

¼ cup yellow mustard

St. Louis Dry Rub (page 213)

¼ cup apple juice

1 cup St. Louis BBQ Sauce (page 212)

The day before you want to eat these beauties, let's start the prep. Slather both sides of the pork ribs with that mustard. It acts as a binder for the rub. Now comes the fun part: the dry rub! Generously sprinkle that rub all over both sides of the ribs, using enough to make sure they're coated in a beautiful, flavorful crust.

Wrap those ribs up tight and stash them in the fridge for at least 24 hours. The longer you marinate, the deeper the flavor gets.

When you are ready to smoke, get your grill or smoker fired up to 350°F and set one side up for indirect heat. Place the ribs bone side down on the indirect heat side of the grill and close the lid. Cook for 30 minutes, letting all that smoky goodness work its magic.

Next, take those ribs off the grill and place them down on aluminum foil. If you're worried about the apple juice spilling, curl up the edges of the foil. Pour that apple juice over the ribs—it's like a flavor bath! Wrap them up tightly. Place the wrapped ribs back on the indirect side of the grill, bump up the temperature to 375°F, and cook for another 30 minutes.

After 30 minutes, turn the heat down to 250°F, unwrap those ribs, and place them back on the grill. Now for the fun part: basting! Brush on the St. Louis BBQ Sauce every 15 minutes for a total of 1 hour, or until the internal temperature of the ribs reaches 195°F (that's the magic number).

Let those ribs rest for 10 minutes (trust us, it's worth it), then slice them up and prepare to be amazed. This is St. Louis–style BBQ at its finest!

COOKING TIME:
4 HOURS
(40 HOURS TOTAL TIME)

SERVES 10

SMOKED TURKEY

Hey, grill masters and Thanksgiving champions! This year, ditch the dry bird and enter the league of epic turkey recipes. We're talkin' perfectly cooked, unbelievably flavorful turkey that's a guaranteed crowd-pleaser. This bird isn't just delicious, it's stunningly beautiful with a gorgeous, even color. Plus, spatchcocking means faster cooking times and easier carving. Basically, it's a Thanksgiving win-win!

We're using a wet brine to infuse the bird with moisture and incredible flavor, making every bite a juicy sensation.

1½ cups kosher salt
½ cup white sugar
2 bay leaves
1 tablespoon whole peppercorns
5 garlic cloves, crushed
1 tablespoon dried rosemary
1 (12-pound) turkey
St. Louis Dry Rub (page 213)
8 tablespoons (1 stick) unsalted butter, melted

Let's brine! Grab a huge pot or bowl and combine 1 gallon of water with the salt, sugar, bay leaves, whole peppercorns, garlic cloves, and rosemary. Stir until all of the salt and sugar dissolve.

To make this easier, we're going to spatchcock the turkey before brining it. Grab those poultry shears and cut along either side of the turkey's backbone. We're removing that bone (save it for gravy later!). Gently press the turkey down flat. This will help it cook evenly and look amazing.

Place the turkey in the brine, making sure the bird is completely submerged. Top it up with more water if needed. Let that turkey soak up all that delicious flavor in the fridge overnight.

The next day, rinse your turkey and pat it dry. An extra step to get crispy skin (if you can wait): place the turkey on a platter in your refrigerator for 8 to 12 hours, uncovered, to dry the skin out fully.

When you are ready to start, get your smoker set at 275°F. We recommend a medium-smoke wood or pellet like pecan, hickory, or even a fruit wood for this turkey. Time to coat that turkey in flavor! Season the underside generously with St. Louis Dry Rub. Then, flip it over. Carefully loosen the skin over the breast meat with your hands.

recipe continues

Just be gentle and avoid any tears. Once the skin is loosened, season that breast meat lightly. Pull the skin back over the breast and season the entire skin all over. Let the turkey sit for at least 15 minutes to let all those seasonings adhere.

Place that seasoned turkey in your smoker and let it get nice and smoky at 275°F. If you're feeling fancy, you can baste the turkey periodically with melted butter for an extra layer of richness. It should take about 3 hours to cook this beautiful bird. Once the internal temperature reaches 160°F in the thickest part of the breast, pull it from the smoker and let it rest for 30 minutes. Carve it up and serve!

COOKING TIME: 25 MINUTES

SERVES 6

BLAZIN' HOT LINK SANDWICH

Calling all grill enthusiasts and lovers of bold flavors! This Blazin' Hot Link Sandwich will tantalize your taste buds and leave you wanting more. We're ditching the cheese for a lighter option, but trust us, the heat and spice will be the stars of the show.

Avocado oil
6 hot link sausages
6 French rolls
Spicy brown mustard
6 dill pickles, sliced lengthwise
Celery salt

Preheat your grill to medium heat. Once your grill is nice and hot, use a kitchen towel to give it a good rub with some avocado oil. We don't want those sausages to stick. Grab those hot links and slice them in half lengthwise, but don't cut them all the way through. Put them face down on the grill and do not move for at least a few minutes. When they begin to char, they will become unstuck from the grill grates. Give them some nice grill marks, and after 5 minutes remove them from the grill and set aside.

Get those French rolls ready by carefully slicing them open along the top, but leave the bottom whole—you want them to hold everything in! Toss them on the grill and give them a little color. Watch them closely and only keep them on the grill for a minute or two.

Once the hot links are cooked to perfection, take those buns off the grill. Add a nice helping of your mustard, then the sausages, and finish with a layer of cool pickles and a little shake of celery salt.

Apple Slaw,
p. 58

Blazin' Hot Link Sandwich, *p. 51*

**COOKING TIME:
2½ HOURS**

SERVES 8

ST. LOUIS PORK STEAKS

Get ready to conquer the legendary St. Louis pork steak with this reverse-seared recipe. We're talking melt-in-your-mouth pork bathed in a smoky, sweet, and tangy BBQ sauce. This ain't just a meal, it's a grilling masterpiece.

8 (1-inch-thick) pork steaks
St. Louis Dry Rub (page 213)
2 cups KC BBQ Sauce (page 221)

Fire it up! Preheat one side of your grill to medium heat. We want the entire grill to be around 225°F when the lid is closed; low and slow is the way to go for this cook. Generously season both sides of those pork steaks with our St. Louis Dry Rub.

Place the seasoned steaks on the cool side of the grill (no direct heat) and close the lid. Let them cook for 2 hours or until they reach an internal temperature of 160°F to 163°F.

Take those cooked steaks off the grill and crank the heat up to high (think 550°F to 600°F). Once the grill is scorching hot, place the steaks back on and sear them for 2 to 3 minutes per side. You're looking for those beautiful grill marks! Flip the steaks and immediately baste them with our KC BBQ Sauce. Let them sear for another 1 to 2 minutes for extra flavor.

Remove the steaks from the grill and let them rest for 5 minutes before serving. This allows the juices to redistribute throughout the meat, resulting in an incredibly tender and flavorful bite. Now go forth and grill with confidence! Your taste buds will thank you.

Budwe
KING OF

COOKING TIME: 1½ HOURS

SERVES 4

RED HOT RIPLETS BEER CAN CHICKEN

We're talking about the legendary beer can chicken, a method that delivers perfectly cooked, unbelievably flavorful poultry every single time. You might be wondering, "Why would a chicken need a beer can?" Well, the answer is simple: moisture and flavor. The beer steams the chicken from the inside out, resulting in incredibly juicy meat. Plus, the seasoning we're using here, Old Vienna Red Hot Riplets, is a St. Louis classic.

1 (4-pound) whole chicken

2 tablespoons avocado oil

3 tablespoons Old Vienna Red Hot Riplets Seasoning

2 tablespoons kosher salt

1 teaspoon freshly ground black pepper

1 (12-ounce) can light beer

First, we're going to prep our chicken. Remove the giblets and neck—nobody wants those! Then, rinse the chicken inside and out and pat it dry. Lightly rub the chicken with the oil, then coat the skin with your Red Hot Riplets Seasoning, salt, and pepper. Don't forget to season inside the cavity as well!

Crack open that beer and take a few big sips (we won't judge). You want the can to be about half full. Place the beer can on a stable surface. Carefully lift the chicken by its legs and position it over the can so the cavity rests on the opening.

Preheat your grill and set it up with one burner off for indirect cooking. It should be around 400°F when the lid is closed. Transfer the chicken-can creation to your grill and place on the indirect side, balancing it on the legs and can like a tripod. Cook over medium-high indirect heat with the lid closed for about 1 hour and 15 minutes. An internal temperature of 165°F in the breast and 180°F in the thigh is what you're aiming for. You can also check for doneness by piercing the thigh with a sharp knife; the juices should run clear.

Take that chicken off the grill and let it rest for 10 minutes before carving. There you have it, folks! A beer can chicken that's easy, delicious, and full of St. Louis flavor.

COOKING TIME:
1¼ HOURS

SERVES 4

APPLE SLAW

Get ready to add a burst of fresh flavor to your next meal with our classic Apple Slaw. We love this recipe because it's simple and adds a nice crunch to your St. Louis BBQ plate.

¼ cup extra-virgin olive oil
1 teaspoon Dijon mustard
1 tablespoon lemon juice
1 tablespoon honey
2 cups shredded red cabbage
8 radishes, chopped
2 medium tart, crisp apples, shredded
1 red onion, chopped or grated
Kosher salt
Freshly ground black pepper

In a large bowl, add the oil, mustard, lemon juice, and honey. Whisk it all together until you have a smooth and creamy dressing. Add the cabbage, radishes, apples, and red onion to the bowl and toss everything together until it's well combined. Season with a heavy pinch of salt and pepper.

Cover the bowl and refrigerate the slaw for at least an hour. This allows the flavors to meld and mellow for a truly delightful taste experience. The slaw can stay chilled for up to a few hours, but be sure to drain any excess liquid before serving if it sits for a longer time.

Right before serving, adjust the seasonings to your preference. A simple yet impressive apple slaw that's perfect for any occasion. So grab your favorite vegetables and get slawin'!

MEMPHIS MAGIC

Dry & Wet to Rock Your Taste Buds

LL
N
DERS
COME
255

FOR OUR THIRD CITY GUIDE, WE'RE ROLLING DEEP INTO the "BBQ Capital of the World," Memphis, Tennessee! Memphis BBQ isn't just food—it's a legacy. From those iconic dry rubs to the mouthwatering Memphis pork, every bite tells a story that's been passed down through generations. Sure, sauce might not always be calling the shots here, but trust us, the flavors born from decades of BBQ tradition? They're the real MVPs, delivering some of the most unforgettable tastes you'll ever experience in the States.

Now, when AC Barbeque sets its sights on a city, we don't just scratch the surface—we dive right in. We wanted the full Memphis experience, the kind you can't find in a guidebook. So, we hit the ground running, from the electric atmosphere of Memphis in May—known to many as the "Super Bowl of Swine"—to those beloved family-run joints and hidden culinary gems scattered across Bluff City.

But hey, don't just take our word for it—come along for the ride! Follow us as we navigate the BBQ-soaked streets of Memphis, sharing insider tips, must-visit spots, and, of course, those finger-licking flavors that make this city a mecca for BBQ lovers everywhere. So, grab your appetite and let's get grilling, because when it comes to BBQ, Memphis is more than just a destination—it's an experience, and trust us, you won't want to miss it!

THE SPOTS

MEMPHIS IN MAY

Known as the "Super Bowl of Swine," the Memphis in May World Championship Barbecue Cooking Contest is a four-day competition that has helped to solidify Memphis's place as a barbeque powerhouse. Pitmasters from all over the world travel to Memphis each year hoping to become the next BBQ World Champion. The contest features championship pork categories of Ribs, Shoulder, and Whole Hog, as well as the ancillary competitions of Hot Wings, Sauce, and "Anything But Pork."

PAYNE'S BAR-B-Q

Since Horton and Flora Payne opened Payne's Bar-B-Q in 1972, the restaurant has become a local obsession. Housed in a humble white cinderblock building (which happens to be a former gas station), Payne's Bar-B-Q smokes its meats in a custom pit built right into the wall. They've been doing barbeque the same way for decades—and that's just how the people of Memphis like it. One of the most popular dishes, the jumbo chopped pork sandwich, is made with pork shoulder slow-roasted in the recessed pit over hickory charcoal. Payne's is also known for their tangy, mild barbeque sauce spiked with mustard and slow-simmered in-house. There's no doubt the food is delicious, but it's Payne's family-run track record that makes it an ideal representative of Memphis BBQ culture.

HELEN'S BAR BQ

You couldn't come to Memphis without making the trek to Helen's in Brownsville. Helen Turner flipped the BBQ scene upside down in 1996. She took that opportunity and ran with it, creating a cult-classic spot where history met in-your-face flavor. Helen became famous in the barbeque world for her old-school open-pit method: just bricks, metal fencing, hot coals, and a whole lot of smoke. Though the restaurant is now closed, Helen's commitment to tradition and her deep love for the craft left a lasting impression. We're grateful we got to witness her passion up close.

COZY CORNER BBQ

Since 1977, Cozy Corner BBQ has served not only some fantastic BBQ but a true taste of Memphis culture as well. An authentic family-owned Memphis institution, they have welcomed thousands of people from around the world to enjoy their cozy hometown vibes and top-tier cuisine. They have been featured in national platforms like *Southern Living* and *Food & Wine*, have written numerous cookbooks, and earned a spot in American Royal's BBQ Hall of Fame. Check 'em out!

CENTRAL BBQ

Central BBQ was born and raised in the fires of barbeque competition—where only the absolute best was good enough. Craig Blondis and Roger Sapp's journey began on the competitive barbeque circuit in the 1980s. Forging a friendship after competing in Memphis in the World Championship Barbecue Cooking Contest and many other BBQ competitions, they decided to join forces. In 2002, their passion for smoky goodness fired up their first location. They've expanded outside Memphis to Nashville, but their commitment remains the same: serving delicious barbeque with a side of friendly service.

POLLARD'S BAR-B-QUE

In 1995, Tarrance Pollard founded Pollard's as a mobile catering business. In 2011, it took its place in the city as a full-on dine-in restaurant. In 2019, Pollard's embraced the steady momentum as the Dallas Cowboys drafted Tony Pollard, Tarrance's son, as a running back. Pollard's has been officially transformed into a major hot spot for everyone to enjoy some great, down South, lip-smacking BBQ!

**COOKING TIME:
8 HOURS
(20½ HOURS TOTAL TIME)**

SERVES 20

PULLED PORK

Calling all BBQ enthusiasts! It's time to get your slow cooker ready for some Memphis-style magic. This legendary pulled pork recipe is about to become your new go-to. This recipe is so simple; you just toss everything in and let the magic happen. Perfect for busy weeknights and relaxed weekend cookouts. And it uses the time-tested method of cider brining to infuse the pork with flavor and moisture. Then, low and slow smoking with hickory chips adds that distinctive smoky depth that true BBQ lovers crave.

1 (8-pound) bone-in pork shoulder roast

1 quart apple cider

Memphis Dry Rub (page 216)

1 yellow onion, chopped

Hamburger buns, for serving

Memphis BBQ Sauce (page 217), for serving

Place that pork shoulder in a large pot. Next, take your quart of apple cider and mix in ¼ cup of your Memphis Dry Rub. Cover the pork shoulder completely with the apple cider mixture. This overnight brine will work its wonders while you sleep. Store in your refrigerator covered.

After 12 hours of brining, remove the pork from the cider and pat it dry. Reserve some of that flavorful cider by pouring it into the water pan for the smoker. Also toss in the chopped onion and a sprinkle of the rub for an extra layer of flavor in the smoke.

Preheat your smoker to 210°F and add some soaked hickory chips for that smoky goodness. Generously coat the pork shoulder with the remaining rub.

Place the seasoned pork shoulder above the water pan and let it smoke for 8 hours, or until it reaches an internal temperature of 200°F. Be sure to keep an eye on the smoker and add more wood chips or liquid as needed.

Once the pork is cooked through, transfer it to a large platter and let it rest for 30 minutes. This allows the juices to redistribute throughout the meat, resulting in an incredibly tender and flavorful pulled pork experience.

Grab your forks and shred that pork! Now you're ready to serve it on hamburger buns with your Memphis BBQ Sauce and any sides your heart desires.

COOKING TIME:
5 HOURS
(9 HOURS TOTAL TIME)

SERVES 8

SMOKED DRY-RUB PORK RIBS

Get ready to experience the magic of Smoked Dry-Rub Pork Ribs with this recipe for fall-off-the-bone deliciousness. They are guaranteed to be a crowd-pleaser! Memphis ribs are all about pure, smoky flavor. No fuss, no muss—just high-quality ingredients and a touch of spice. So fire up your smoker, grab your favorite Memphis-style rub, and get ready to experience BBQ bliss!

2 (2-pound) racks pork loin ribs or baby back ribs, membranes removed

Memphis Dry Rub (page 216)

2 cups apple juice

½ cup red wine vinegar

½ cup olive oil

Get your hands on some beautiful pork loin ribs. Wash and pat the ribs dry. Moisture is the enemy of a good dry rub! Use enough Memphis Dry Rub to generously coat the ribs on both sides. The beauty of this recipe is that you don't need any oil or binder—the rub will work its magic on its own.

Let the ribs rest in the refrigerator for at least 4 hours. This allows the dry rub to penetrate the meat, infusing it with flavor. Pull the ribs out about an hour before you want to start smoking.

Fire up your smoker to 250°F and add some hickory wood for that smoky goodness. Place the seasoned ribs on the smoker. Unlike some methods, we won't be wrapping these ribs. Instead, we'll be basting them for added moisture and flavor.

While the ribs are starting to cook, let's make the mop sauce. In a large bowl, combine the apple juice, vinegar, oil, and 2 tablespoons of the Memphis Dry Rub.

Starting at the hour-and-a-half mark, baste the ribs every 45 minutes for the next three hours with the mopping sauce. You'll know they are ready because they will begin to get dry, especially down the middle. This helps keep them moist and adds another layer of deliciousness.

The smoking process should take around 4½ hours, resulting in ribs that are tender with a nice snap. If you can tear them apart at the bone with your bare hands, they're ready.

For that truly authentic Memphis-style presentation, give the ribs a final dusting of the Memphis Dry Rub right before serving.

in the
Helen's
BBQ

Payne's BAR-B-Q
B-B-Q PLATES
B-B-Q SANDWICHES
RIBS
WHOLE SHOULDERS
BEANS
POLISH SAUSAGES

**COOKING TIME:
30 MINUTES
(9 HOURS TOTAL TIME)**

SERVES 4

PORK T-BONES

Woo! These Pork T-Bones are sure to elevate your next cookout. These beauties are packed with flavor and juicy tenderness because we're going to brine the pork, ensuring every bit is juicy and delicious. The T-bone cut offers the best of both worlds: the tenderloin (like a pork filet mignon) and the flavorful loin.

1 gallon distilled white vinegar

1 lemon, thinly sliced

2 cups white sugar

½ cup freshly ground black pepper

⅓ cup cayenne pepper

1¼ tablespoons crushed red pepper flakes

Memphis Dry Rub (page 216)

4 (8-ounce) pork T-bone steaks (1 inch thick)

Canola oil, for oiling the grill

In a large pot, warm the vinegar over low heat. Once it reaches 150°F, add the lemon slices and simmer for 10 minutes. Then, whisk in the sugar, black pepper, cayenne pepper, and red pepper flakes. Cook until the sugar dissolves and the mixture reaches 190°F. Remove from the heat, let it cool completely, and remove the lemon slices. Whisk in the Memphis Dry Rub a spoonful at a time until the consistency looks like a spicy vinegar.

Put your pork T-bone steaks in a large resealable plastic bag and cover them completely in your brine mixture. Save at least ½ cup of the brine in a separate container for serving. Marinate the steaks for at least 8 hours in the refrigerator. Remove the steaks from the resealable plastic bag and save the marinade for mopping; you'll need at least ¼ cup.

Preheat your grill with your burners on medium-high heat. Lightly oil the grill grates with canola oil. Sear the T-bones for 8 minutes per side, mopping them with marinade occasionally, every 2 minutes or so. To ensure the meat gets cooked through, stand the T-bones upright for an additional 4 minutes. Transfer the cooked T-bones to a platter. There you have it, folks! Serve with the ½ cup of brine mixture you saved before marinating. You better grab one of these fast; there won't be any left.

COOKING TIME:
30 MINUTES

SERVES 4

BBQ SPAGHETTI

Memphis's most unique barbeque creation might just be BBQ Spaghetti. Forget about grilling noodles or serving barbeque and spaghetti side-by-side. This dish is a symphony of flavors that has the meat right in it, a true Memphis original.

This dish has the perfect balance of sweet from the BBQ sauce and tang from the tomato sauce, creating a flavor explosion in every bite. Succulent pulled pork adds a meaty layer of deliciousness, making this dish a complete meal without any extras.

1 cup Memphis BBQ Sauce (page 217)

1½ cups marinara sauce

1 pound Pulled Pork (page 65)

Kosher salt

1 (16-ounce) package spaghetti

Memphis Dry Rub (page 216)

In a large pot, combine the Memphis BBQ Sauce, marinara sauce, and pulled pork over medium-low heat. Stir it all together to create a flavor base that will have your taste buds singing. While the sauce simmers, bring a large pot of salted water to a boil. Cook the spaghetti according to package directions for al dente.

Drain the cooked spaghetti and add it to the pot with the simmering sauce mixture. Continue to heat everything over medium-low heat, stirring frequently, until the spaghetti, sauce, and meat are all happy and heated through, about 5 minutes.

Plate your BBQ spaghetti masterpiece and sprinkle each serving with a generous dusting of our Memphis Dry Rub. This adds a final touch of smoky Memphis magic. Serve this flavor-packed dish and watch your family devour it! BBQ Spaghetti is the perfect weeknight meal or delicious side dish that's guaranteed to satisfy.

COOKING TIME:
20 MINUTES

SERVES 8

HUSH PUPPIES

Calling all fans of down-home cooking! These bite-size puffs of goodness are guaranteed to steal the show at your next gathering. Don't let their humble appearance fool you. These puppies pack a flavor punch with a slightly sweet cornmeal batter that's light and fluffy on the inside and crisp and golden brown on the outside. And they are the perfect appetizer or side dish for any meal. Pair them with your favorite barbeque, seafood, or fried chicken for a finger-lickin' good time.

1 cup stone-ground cornmeal
½ cup all-purpose flour
2 tablespoons white sugar
1½ teaspoons baking powder
½ teaspoon kosher salt, plus more for finishing
¼ teaspoon cayenne pepper
1 large egg
¾ cup whole buttermilk
½ small yellow onion, grated
Vegetable oil

In a large bowl, whisk together the cornmeal, flour, sugar, baking powder, salt, and cayenne pepper. In a separate bowl, our wet ingredients are going to have a party. Grab your egg and buttermilk and give them a good whisk. Then, mosey on over to the dry ingredients and add the wet crew, along with the grated onion. Stir it all together until it's a happy, combined batter.

Heat up about 2 inches of vegetable oil in a Dutch oven over medium-high heat. You want your oil to be around 375°F. Now for the fun part! Carefully drop heaping tablespoons of batter into the hot oil using a spoon. Don't overcrowd the pan, and fry those puppies for 2 minutes each, turning them halfway through with a spatula, until they're golden brown and irresistible. Once they're golden and crispy, take your hush puppies out of the oil and salt them. Let them rest on a wire rack lined with paper towels to drain any excess oil.

COOKING TIME:
30 MINUTES

SERVES 4

GREEN BEANS

Looking for a way to turn those everyday green beans into something truly extraordinary? Look no further than these green beans. This recipe is all about achieving that perfect balance of textures. We're talking crisp-tender green beans that snap with every bite, all cloaked in a blanket of irresistibly crunchy breadcrumbs. And best of all: This recipe comes together in 30 minutes, making it the perfect weeknight side dish or an elegant dinner party side.

1 pound green beans, washed and ends removed

2 tablespoons bacon drippings (salted butter works but doesn't compare to the bacon flavor)

¼ cup breadcrumbs

Kosher salt

Freshly ground black pepper

Bring a large pot of water to a boil. Once it's boiling, add the green beans and cook for just 3 minutes. We want them crisp-tender, not mushy! Immediately drain the beans and plunge them into a bowl of ice water to stop the cooking process. This keeps them bright green and extra crisp. Once the beans have cooled, take them out of the ice bath and pat them dry with paper towels. Extra moisture is the enemy of crispness!

Heat up your bacon drippings or butter in a frying pan over medium-high heat. Add the green beans to the hot fat and let them cook for about 5 minutes, tossing them around occasionally, until they're browned on all sides.

Turn the heat down to medium and add the breadcrumbs. Toss the beans with the breadcrumbs until they're evenly coated. Let the breadcrumbs toast up for a bit, adding an extra layer of flavor and crunch. Season with a pinch of salt and a pinch of pepper to taste.

Plate your gorgeous green beans and savor that satisfying crunch in every bite.

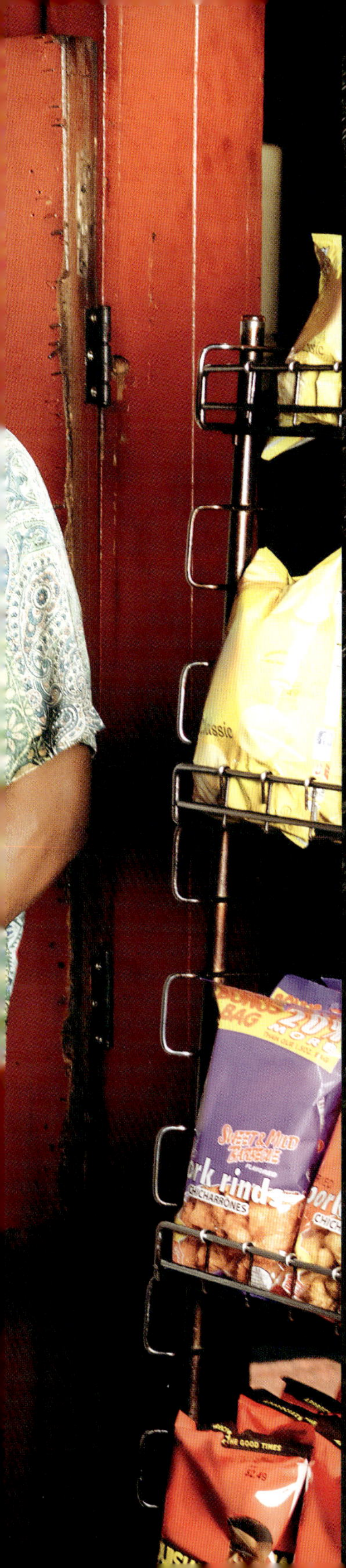

CAROLINA CLASSICS

Whole Hog Versus Red Sauce

FIRE UP YOUR GRILLS AND GET READY TO SHOUT "YEEHAW!" because we're diving headfirst into the sizzling world of Carolina BBQ. Yep, we're talking about the Carolinas, where BBQ isn't just food—it's a way of life, steeped in tradition and served with a side of Southern hospitality.

Now, let's set the record straight: Carolina BBQ is far from one-dimensional. This is a culinary landscape where whole hogs are worshipped, mustard-based sauces reign supreme, and every pitmaster worth their salt has a secret recipe up their sleeve. From the vinegary tang of Eastern North Carolina to the mustardy kick of South Carolina, the Carolinas offer a smorgasbord of flavors that'll make your taste buds do a happy dance.

Here at AC Barbeque, we've embarked on a flavorful expedition through the Carolinas, rubbing shoulders with BBQ royalty, uncovering hidden gems, and, of course, indulging in endless BBQ feasts. We've sat down with legendary pitmasters, swapped stories with local BBQ enthusiasts, and even picked up a few smoking tips along the way. And now, we're bringing all that juicy knowledge straight to you!

This Carolina BBQ chapter is your all-access pass to the heart and soul of Southern BBQ. We'll guide you through our top picks—the places that encapsulate the true AC spirit—where BBQ is more than just food, it's a celebration of family, community, and the art of slow-cooked perfection. So, grab your bibs and get ready to dig in, because we're about to take you on a BBQ journey you won't soon forget!

THE SPOTS

RODNEY SCOTT'S BBQ

Rodney Scott's BBQ, founded by the James Beard Award–winning pitmaster Rodney Scott, is the brainchild of the legendary pitmaster himself. This place is a temple of whole-hog barbeque, where each succulent piece of meat is cooked low and slow over wood-fired pits until it's packed with smoky goodness. It's not just barbeque, it's an experience—a journey through the rich history and soulful flavors of Southern cooking.

RED BRIDGES BARBECUE LODGE

Red Bridges Barbecue Lodge is a family-owned treasure that's been serving up mouthwatering barbeque since 1946. Imagine tender pork shoulders, drenched in a tangy vinegar-based sauce, paired with hush puppies so good they'll make you wanna dance. It's classic North Carolina barbeque at its finest, served with a side of Southern charm that keeps folks coming back for generations.

LEXINGTON BARBECUE

Let's talk about Lexington Barbecue, or "the Honeymonk" as the locals lovingly call it. This Lexington, North Carolina, legend is famous for its chopped pork sandwiches topped with a vinegar-based "dip" that strikes the perfect balance between spicy and sweet. It's as addictive as it is delicious, and it's no wonder folks line up around the block to get their Lexington Barbecue fix.

STAMEY'S BARBECUE

Moving on to Stamey's Barbecue in Greensboro, North Carolina, where tradition meets taste in the most mouthwatering way. Since the 1930s, Stamey's has been serving up Eastern-style barbeque that's pit-cooked to perfection and slathered in a zesty vinegar-pepper sauce. It's a taste of history with every bite, and it's guaranteed to leave you craving more.

GRADY'S BBQ

Last but certainly not least, let's shine a spotlight on Grady's BBQ in Dudley, North Carolina, a hidden gem that's worth the journey. Here, you'll find wood-smoked barbeque that's as authentic as it gets, paired with homemade sides that'll make you feel right at home. It's Southern hospitality served on a plate, and it's the kind of place where memories are made.

COOKING TIME:
$1\frac{3}{4}$ HOURS

SERVES 6

COLLARDS
WITH SMOKED TURKEY WINGS

Collards with Smoked Turkey Wings is one of Anthony's favorite dishes, and we can't wait to take you on a trip to flavortown. Get ready for a taste explosion of tender greens, smoky goodness, and all the soulful comfort-food vibes you can handle.

Olive oil

½ yellow onion, diced

3 garlic cloves, diced

3 cups chicken broth

1 teaspoon crushed red pepper flakes

4 smoked turkey wings (about 3 pounds total)

1 bunch collard greens, washed

Kosher salt

Freshly ground black pepper

Hot sauce, to taste

In a large pot, heat up enough olive oil to just coat the bottom of the pan over medium heat. Add the yellow onion and garlic and cook, stirring, until they're nice and soft, 5 to 8 minutes.

Pour in that chicken broth and add the red pepper flakes and turkey wings. Bring it to a boil, then reduce the heat. Cover and let it simmer for about 20 minutes. This step is key for infusing the broth with all that smoky turkey flavor.

Finally, it's time for the collard greens! Add them to the pot and give everything a good stir. Put the cover back on and simmer for 50 minutes or until the greens are tender to your liking.

Once the greens are cooked through, taste your creation and season with salt and pepper. A few drops of hot sauce are also a welcome addition for those who like a little kick! Serve to your favorite friends.

Collards with Smoked Turkey Wings, p. 85

The Coleslaw, p. 101

Fried Catfish, *p. 97*

COOKING TIME:
12 HOURS
(AT LEAST 24 HOURS TOTAL TIME)

SERVES 12

LEXINGTON PORK SANDWICH
WITH PLENTY OF OUTSIDE BROWN

We're talkin' real-deal, slow-smoked, melt-in-your-mouth deliciousness here, folks. Forget those quick and easy recipes that leave you with a pale imitation of BBQ. This is the ultimate guide to smoked pulled pork perfection, from choosing the meat to pulling it apart with your bare hands (or fancy claws; no judgment). Pork butt, also known as Boston butt, is our champion for this recipe. It's a forgiving cut that's hard to mess up, ideal for smoking beginners. Plus, it's perfect for feeding a crowd. While this recipe isn't a race, you can expect to spend a good ten to twelve hours cooking a pork butt. It's a low and slow process, but the reward is well worth the wait!

1 (5-pound) pork butt

3 teaspoons kosher salt

⅓ cup Put Me on Everything Rub (page 203)

12 potato buns

1 cup Lexington, North Carolina, BBQ Sauce (page 219)

Let's get this pork butt prepped: We want a beautiful bark, not greasy meat. Trim most of the fat, leaving a thin layer (about ¼ inch) for flavor. Don't worry about it all rendering—it won't penetrate the meat anyway.

We're going to dry brine. Season the pork butt with salt and refrigerate for 12 to 24 hours. This dry brining allows the salt to penetrate for extra flavor. Just before smoking, lightly wet the surface with water and sprinkle on your Put Me on Everything Rub.

Prepare your smoker or grill for indirect heat cooking at 225°F. Add a few ounces of dry wood chips for that smoky goodness. Once your smoker reaches temperature, insert a digital thermometer probe into the center of the pork butt, avoiding the bone. This lets you monitor the internal temperature without opening the smoker.

Place the pork butt directly on the smoker grate (not in a pan) to allow a flavorful bark to develop on all sides. Let it smoke uninterrupted, checking on your smoker every hour to maintain a temperature between 225°F and 250°F. Don't stress if it goes a little higher—pork butts are forgiving. Add a few more ounces of wood chips during the first two hours for that initial smoky kick. Remember, we want a pleasant smoke flavor, not for it to be overpowering.

Around 150°F, you might hit a stall where the temperature seems to stop climbing. This is normal! It's just science: Moisture evaporation cools the meat as the hot air warms it. Just ride it out, and soon you'll be rewarded with a beautiful bark. As the temperature reaches 170°F, the collagen in the meat starts to melt, making it tender and juicy. Keep cooking past this point.

When the internal temperature reaches 200°F after 8 to 12 hours, it's time to check for doneness. The exterior should be dark brown (don't worry, it's not burnt!), with glistening fat and a possible pink sheen on gas cookers. If there's a bone, it should wiggle and feel like it can come out easily. No bone? Use a fork; if it turns easily with minimal pressure, you're good to go.

If you're not quite ready to serve, you can hold the pork on the smoker (heat off) or in your oven at 170°F for up to an hour. For longer holding times, wrap it tightly in foil to prevent drying.

About 30 minutes before serving, transfer the pork butt to a pan to catch any drippings. Now, the fun part! Use claws, gloves, or forks to pull the pork apart, discarding any large fat chunks. We recommend pulling by hand to retain moisture, but slicing or chopping is also an option. Remember, those flavorful crusty outside bits are called outside brown, and they are gold. Distribute them evenly throughout the pulled pork for maximum deliciousness or hold them on the side if you want to add them to the tops of your sandwiches.

Pile your pork high on your potato buns and top with your Lexington, North Carolina, BBQ Sauce. The leftovers are perfect for anything you can think of, like pizza, tacos, or egg rolls. The possibilities are endless.

COOKING TIME: 3½ HOURS

SERVES 6

SMOKED PRIME RIB

Craving a showstopping centerpiece for your next gathering? Look no further than this epic Smoked Prime Rib recipe. We'll guide you through the process of slow smoking for incredible flavor.

1 (4-pound) prime rib roast
Kosher salt
Freshly ground black pepper
Lexington, North Carolina, BBQ Sauce (page 219)

Get your smoker preheated to 225°F. While it's warming up, prep your prime rib. Sprinkle the meat aggressively with equal parts salt and pepper.

Place the roast on the smoker and close the lid. Smoke it low and slow for about 1 hour. The meat will have browned. Mop the meat with your Lexington, North Carolina, BBQ Sauce. Turn it over and mop the other side.

Close your smoker and cook until the roast reaches an internal temperature of 125°F for rare, 135°F for medium rare, or 145°F for medium. This should take 40 minutes per pound, so 2½ to 3 hours overall. When the prime rib is cooked to your liking, take it off the smoker and cover it with foil on a cutting board. Let it rest for 20 minutes. Then carve and serve with more Lexington, North Carolina, BBQ Sauce on the side.

COOKING TIME:
3 HOURS
(5 HOURS TOTAL TIME)

SERVES 6

SPARE RIBS

We're talkin' Carolina-style perfection—smoky, tangy, and fall-off-the-bone tender. Get ready to impress your guests with this recipe that's easy to prepare and delivers a showstopping presentation with its deep, mahogany shine.

3 (2-pound) slabs pork spare ribs, membranes removed

Put Me on Everything Rub (page 203)

3 cups East Carolina Vinegar Sauce (page 220)

Season each pork spare rib slab with the Put Me on Everything Rub. Make sure you get them completely covered. Let those ribs rest in the fridge for at least 2 hours. Pull them out of the fridge and then let's start our grill.

Fire up your grill to 250°F. Place the seasoned ribs on the grill bone side down, with the fatty end toward the middle of the grill because it's hotter. Close the grill and cook. You are looking for caramelization before you flip them. That should take around 90 minutes.

Next, open the grill and we're going to mop with our East Carolina Vinegar Sauce. Mop the top of the meat, flip the meat over, and mop the meat again. Close the grill and bring the temperature back up to 250°F. Cook the ribs until this side looks caramelized, which should take another 90 minutes. When you pick up one of the slabs, it should sag, and if it tears slightly, that's a good sign that your ribs are done. Take them off the grill and cut them up. Serve with the rest of your East Carolina Vinegar Sauce. These will take you to Carolina heaven!

Pour the
COALS to it

COALS to

COOKING TIME: 25 MINUTES

SERVES 4

FRIED CATFISH

Craving a crispy, flavorful fish sandwich? Look no further than this recipe for perfectly crisp catfish fillets coated in a crave-worthy cornmeal crust. It's a breeze to make and delivers delicious results in under 30 minutes.

2 cups finely ground cornmeal

1 cup all-purpose flour

2 teaspoons Old Vienna Red Hot Riplets Seasoning (you can use Old Bay seasoning if you would like)

2 teaspoons cayenne pepper, divided

1 teaspoon freshly ground black pepper

3 pounds catfish fillets

Vegetable oil

1 teaspoon kosher salt

In a bowl, combine the cornmeal, flour, Red Hot Riplets Seasoning, 1 teaspoon of the cayenne pepper, and the black pepper. Coat each catfish fillet in the cornmeal mixture.

Set up your paper towel draining station next to a Dutch oven on your range. Add enough vegetable oil to the Dutch oven to reach a depth of 2 inches. Heat the oil to 350°F.

Carefully place the coated catfish fillets in the hot oil and fry them in batches. They should be golden brown on the bottom after about 3 minutes. Flip and fry for another 3 minutes. Once they are cooked, remove them from the oil and drain on paper towels. Don't forget to season them with a pinch of salt and the remaining teaspoon of cayenne pepper while they're hot for that Carolina flavor!

COOKING TIME:
45 MINUTES

SERVES 4

ANTHONY'S WINGS

These wings are about to become the MVP of your next barbeque. Whether you're a seasoned smoker pro or a grill master in the making, this recipe delivers smoky, flavorful chicken wings with a perfectly crisp finish. And Anthony can't get enough of them.

2 pounds chicken wings
Kosher salt
Freshly ground black pepper
East Carolina Vinegar Sauce (page 220)

Build a small fire in your grill, leaving one side free of coals. If you're using a gas grill, turn one burner to low, then preheat with the cover closed for 15 minutes.

Time to add some smokiness! Toss 2 to 3 handfuls of water-soaked wood chips (apple, cherry, or hickory are all great choices) onto the coals for charcoal grills. For gas grills, create a foil pouch using two large pieces of foil. Place 2 to 3 handfuls of soaked wood chips inside, fold it shut, and poke a few holes on top with a fork. Place this pouch on your hottest burner.

Generously sprinkle your chicken wings with salt and pepper. Now, place them on the cool side of the grill, opposite the wood chips. By now, you should see smoke billowing! Cover the grill and let the wings smoke their magic for 15 minutes.

Time to crank up the flavor! Uncover the grill and move the chicken directly over the coals (charcoal grills) or to a low-flame area (gas grills). No matter which method you choose, baste those wings frequently with your East Carolina Vinegar Sauce and turn them often for even cooking.

Once the wings are golden brown, perfectly crisp, and cooked through, remove them from the heat and transfer them to a warm platter. Get ready for a round of applause from your hungry guests!

COOKING TIME:
$1\frac{1}{2}$ HOURS

SERVES 6

THE COLESLAW

Ditch the store-bought stuff and whip up The Coleslaw in minutes. We're talkin' a flavor explosion made with ingredients you probably already have on hand. No fancy trips to the grocery store required! Don't tell anybody, but this also works if you just want to make the dressing and toss it with a bag of coleslaw mix from the supermarket. It will add a creamy and tangy punch to any crunchy vegetable you put it on.

1 cup mayonnaise
2 tablespoons white sugar
Juice of 1 lemon
1 tablespoon white vinegar
Freshly ground black pepper
Kosher salt
3 cups finely shredded green cabbage
2 cups finely shredded purple cabbage
1 cup finely shredded carrot

Throw your mayo, sugar, lemon juice, vinegar, a pinch of pepper, and a pinch of salt into a small bowl and give it a good whisk until it's smooth, creamy, and ready to take your coleslaw to the next level.

Add your green cabbage, purple cabbage, and carrot to a large bowl. Pour the dressing over it and give it a good toss to combine. Cover and refrigerate for at least 1 hour. Serve—this is one coleslaw that will not be left after the cookout.

BARBEQUE

KANSAS CITY
KICKIN'
Slow & Thick
BBQ Blowout

FIRE UP THOSE SMOKERS AND GET READY TO SHOUT "HEY, Y'ALL!" because we're plunging into the tantalizing world of Kansas City BBQ. That's right, Kansas City, the barbeque mecca where every bite is a flavor-packed journey through smoky, saucy goodness, is calling our names.

Now, forget everything you thought you knew about barbeque, because Kansas City is where traditions meet innovation in the most delicious way possible. Here, it's not just about one type of meat or one style of sauce—it's an all-out BBQ extravaganza, featuring everything from succulent pork ribs and melt-in-your-mouth brisket to juicy chicken and beyond. And let's not forget about that iconic, thick, sweet and tangy tomato-based sauce that's practically a food group of its own!

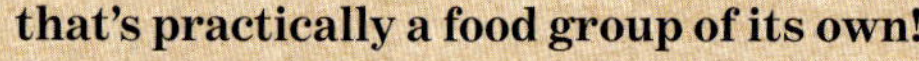

We've been on a lip-smacking quest through the heart of Kansas City's BBQ scene. We've rubbed shoulders with legendary pitmasters, sampled the city's most iconic dishes, and indulged in some seriously mouthwatering feasts. We've laughed, we've learned, and, most importantly, we've eaten a lot.

This AC Kansas City BBQ chapter is your golden ticket to the ultimate barbeque adventure. KC is a place where BBQ is a celebration of flavor, community, and the pure joy of cooking over an open flame. So grab your napkins and loosen those belts, because we're about to dive into a BBQ experience that's as bold, flavorful, and unforgettable as Kansas City itself.

THE SPOTS

ARTHUR BRYANT'S BARBEQUE

First up, we've got Arthur Bryant's Barbeque, a Jazz District gem that's a favorite haunt for locals, tourists, and even Beltway politicians. This iconic spot, hailed by writer Calvin Trillin as "the single best restaurant in the world," hasn't changed much over the years—think Formica tables, framed newspaper clippings, and greasy floor tiles. While they're famous for their burnt ends, the real star of the show these days is their lean brisket sandwich, slathered in AB's distinctive brick-red, vinegar-bright sauce. It's a flavor experience that sparks endless culinary debates, and trust us, you won't find sauce like this anywhere else.

JONES BAR-B-Q

Next, let's talk about Jones Bar-B-Q, a family-owned roadside joint owned by sisters Deborah ("Little") Jones and Mary ("Shorty") Jones Mosley. They are the queens of ribs, rib tip sandwiches, and burnt ends. This no-frills spot might be small and sun-soaked, but what it lacks in size, it more than makes up for in flavor and innovation. From their iconic barbeque vending machine to their mouthwatering turkey sandwiches, the Jones sisters keep things fresh, and the city keeps getting better for it.

GATES BAR-B-Q

Moving on to Gates Bar-B-Q: This local institution has been serving up true, crispy-crackly burnt ends since 1946, and they don't take shortcuts when it comes to flavor. Whether you're indulging in their burnt-end sandwich or squeezing their beloved house sauce over everything, Gates is all about that perfect balance of sweet, vinegar, smoke, and heat. With cozy brown booths and a quiet bar, the Main Street location is a favorite spot to soak in the casual vibes and savor every bite.

JOE'S KANSAS CITY BAR-B-QUE

Now let's talk about Joe's Kansas City Bar-B-Que, where barbeque dreams come to life inside an old gas station. Named one of Anthony Bourdain's "thirteen places to eat before you die," Joe's is famous for its top-notch beef ribs, burnt ends, and thin-sliced brisket. If you want to eat like a local, call ahead for carryout and don't miss out on their seasoned fries or dirty rice. It's a culinary experience that lives up to the hype, and trust us, the wait is well worth it.

LC'S BAR-B-Q

Last but certainly not least, let's dive into LC's Bar-B-Q, a classic counter-service restaurant that's a must-visit for barbeque purists. With a jet-black three-tiered pit that's always bustling with whole briskets, racks of ribs, and hams, LC's is all about keeping things authentic. Stick to the classics here—burnt ends, brisket, and thick-cut fries—and you'll see why this place has been a KC favorite for years. Run by LC Richardson's granddaughter, the recipes and that iconic pit remain unchanged, preserving the rich barbeque legacy that KC is known for.

**COOKING TIME:
10 HOURS
(AT LEAST 14 HOURS
TOTAL TIME)**

SERVES 8

BURNT ENDS

In the smoky world of BBQ, burnt ends weren't always the kings of the castle they are today. Believe it or not, these crispy, finger-lickin' nuggets of beefy goodness used to be just the scraps—the overcooked edges of briskets that only the lucky pitmasters got to enjoy.

But times have changed! Now burnt ends are BBQ hall-of-famers, usually made from that prime cut, the brisket point. This recipe here is your golden ticket to burnt-end bliss. We're talkin' smoky, melt-in-your-mouth cubes of pure beefy goodness. We'll show you everything you need to know, from pickin' out the perfect cut to crafting the ultimate bite-size beef bombs. Get ready to turn these once-discarded leftovers into the MVPs of your next BBQ bash.

1 (6-pound) brisket point

Kosher salt

Put Me on Everything Rub (page 203)

¼ cup beef broth

¼ cup KC BBQ Sauce (page 221)

Trim the fat off your brisket point like a champ. Save those trimmings; we'll need them to finish the dish later. Cover that bad boy in a nice layer of salt and store it in your refrigerator overnight (4 hours minimum if you're short on time). We want that flavor to seep in deep.

Rub-a-dub-dub! After salting, get generous with the Put Me on Everything Rub and massage it all over the meat. Keep that brisket out until it's smokin' time. Remember, chilled meat attracts more smoke! Grab your remote digital thermometer and stick that probe right in the thickest part of the meat.

Get your smoker with a water pan preheated for indirect cooking. We're talkin' low and slow here. Aim for 225°F. It might drop a bit when you add the meat; that's cool. Place the brisket on the cooker right above the water pan and add some wood chunks for that smoky goodness. Replenish the wood every 30 minutes or so for the first 2 hours. Keep that water pan full! Do not let it dry out. Patience is a virtue! Don't be tempted to mess with the meat. No moppin', bastin', or spritzin' needed. We want that perfect bark to form.

After 3 hours, check the color of your meat. If it's different on top and bottom, give it a flip. Otherwise, let it be.

Once that internal temp hits 155°F and you've got a nice dark color, it's time to wrap that brisket up tight in foil (double layer for good measure). Swaddle the meat in foil, leaving an opening at the top. Pour

the broth into the opening, then securely seal the opening with foil. This keeps the meat moist and prevents a stall in the cooking process. Put the wrapped brisket back on the cooker for indirect heat and cook until we hit 195°F.

When it reaches 195°F, carefully remove the brisket from the foil, saving those drippings for later. Let it cool for 5 minutes. Cut that point into 1-inch cubes. Save any fatty bits for a hardworking BBQ snack right there (we won't judge). Dust those cubes with some leftover rub and a sprinkle of brown sugar. Toss them on the grill topper on the hot side of the grill to caramelize the sugar.

In a frying pan, take that beautiful beef fat you trimmed earlier and set it over the hot side of the grill. Move the cubes to the pan and gently fry them until they are crunchy on the outside. Get ready to create some crispy, finger-lickin' magic! Drain the fat and add equal parts of your KC BBQ sauce and beef broth drippings. Let those cubes sizzle and soak up all that flavor and stir every 2 minutes or so. Don't burn 'em, though! When they're done, serve these bad boys immediately before they go soft.

COOKING TIME:
15 MINUTES

MAKES 2 SANDWICHES

KC BACON, LETTUCE, AND TOMATO

We're talkin' a flavor explosion that'll have your taste buds doin' a touchdown dance! This recipe is all about balance, just like a well-thrown Patrick Mahomes pass. We got that lusciousness from mayo, the crunch from toasted bread, and the smoky, salty goodness of the shoulder bacon, a Kansas City legend itself. This bacon is wider and meatier than traditional bacon. It's also known as cottage bacon.

8 slices shoulder bacon (gotta be that KC specialty!)

4 slices thick white bread

Mayonnaise

Maldon sea salt

Freshly ground black pepper

2 juicy heirloom tomatoes, cored and sliced thin

6 butter lettuce leaves

Grab your skillet and crank up the heat to medium. Fry that shoulder bacon in batches until it's golden brown and looking real good (about 4 minutes per batch). Once it's done, set it aside on a plate over paper towels.

Toast those bread slices until they're golden brown and crispy. Don't skimp on the toasting! Spread a generous layer of mayo on one side of each toast. Give it a little hit of Maldon salt and black pepper. Time to layer! Divide those tomatoes between two slices of toast. Top them off with some fresh butter lettuce.

Now comes the main event! Lay that crispy shoulder bacon on the remaining slices of toast. Give your sandwich a gentle squeeze to hold it all together. Slice that bad boy in half and get ready to devour it! Don't wait too long to eat this masterpiece. You want that bacon nice and warm for maximum flavor impact!

COOKING TIME: 3 HOURS

SERVES 6

KC BAKED BEANS

These ain't yo grandma's baked beans. We're talkin' a taste sensation that's sweeter, smokier, and guaranteed to have your guests singin' your praises! Now, don't let the ingredient list scare ya—this recipe comes together in a flash. Think of it like a flavor party in a pot: the more ingredients, the merrier! Besides, anything with bacon is a guaranteed win, right?

Wanna take these beans to the next level? Channel your inner pitmaster. Here's a secret weapon used by some of the best BBQ joints: leftover ribs. Take that smoky goodness from the bones and toss it in the pot. You can even add scraps from other meats for an extra bold kick. Just be careful not to overdo the smoke. Trust us, these beans are gonna be the MVP of your next cookout.

3 strips thick-cut bacon

1 yellow onion, chopped

1 red bell pepper, seeded and chopped

½ jalapeño, seeded and chopped

2 (15-ounce) cans cannellini beans, rinsed and drained

⅓ cup KC BBQ Sauce (page 221)

4 leftover KC Ribs (page 115), removed from the bone (optional)

2 tablespoons molasses

2 ounces bourbon

1 teaspoon ground mustard

Kosher salt

Freshly ground black pepper

Fire up your Dutch oven. Cook that bacon over medium heat until it's getting nice and brown. Once it's golden, take it out and drain on some paper towels. Don't toss the fat just yet; we'll use it for extra flavor!

Toss the onion, bell pepper, and jalapeño in the pot with that reserved bacon fat and cook them until they're softened up. Keep an eye on them and add a splash of water if the bits on the bottom start to burn. Now comes the fun part! Pour in 3 cups of water, then add the beans, KC BBQ sauce, rib meat (if using), molasses, bourbon, mustard, and that delicious bacon, and give it a good stir.

You can cook these beans on your smoker by putting that pot under the meat that you might be preparing at the same time for 2 hours at 225°F. Let those smoky drippings infuse the beans with flavor! Or you can simmer them in your slow cooker for about 2 hours. If you want to be boring, you can bring them to a boil on your stovetop and then reduce the heat to a simmer and cook for 30 minutes, stirring occasionally. Don't be boring!

Once the beans are nice and tender, give them a taste test. Add kosher salt and freshly ground black pepper if you'd like. Time to adjust the flavors to your liking. Want it spicier? Add hot sauce. Thicker? Let it simmer longer. Thinner? Add a splash of water. Once you've got the perfect flavor balance, serve those beans hot and enjoy.

LODGE

KC Ribs, p. 115

COOKING TIME:
6 HOURS
(9 HOURS TOTAL TIME)

SERVES 6

KC RIBS

These ain't yo average ribs, fam. We're talkin' fall-off-the-bone perfection, smothered in our famous KC BBQ sauce. This recipe is all about that smoky, sweet goodness that'll have you dreamin' of competition BBQ pits.

2 (3-pound) racks St. Louis–cut ribs, membranes removed

Memphis Dry Rub (page 216)

KC BBQ Sauce (page 221)

Rinse those ribs and score the surface if you can't remove the membrane for better fat rendering. Apply that Memphis Dry Rub generously, coating all surfaces. If you can give the spices and salt an hour or two to work their magic (dry brining), that would be ideal.

Preheat your smoker or grill for indirect cooking at 225°F (low and slow is key for tender perfection). Add some wood chunks for that smoky goodness. Place the ribs meat-side up on the smoker or grill, close the lid, and relax! You can add more wood after 30 minutes, but resist the urge to overdo it. Patience is a virtue.

The big wait: These suckers will take about 6 hours. If your slabs are thick, expect them to take longer. Get a chair and sit your ass down. You'll be able to watch *Barbershop* at least two times, if not three, if you need some pure entertainment.

To check for doneness, use the bend test. Gently pick up the ribs with tongs and bounce them. If the surface cracks slightly, they're ready. This is one of the only meats where thermometers aren't your friend; the meat is too thin.

Brush on your KC BBQ Sauce for a final touch of sweetness and cook for another 15 minutes. Slice the ribs between the bones and admire that beautiful smoke ring. Plate them up and prepare for applause from your hungry audience.

COOKING TIME: 10 MINUTES

SERVES 4

CHEESY CORN

Looking for a side dish that's both easy and insanely delicious? Look no further than this amazing Cheesy Corn recipe! It's ready in just ten minutes, and we guarantee it'll become a new family favorite. Plain corn? Never heard of her!

2 cups cooked corn kernels (from about 4 ears of corn)

2 tablespoons salted butter, melted

Kosher salt

Freshly ground black pepper

1 cup shredded cheddar cheese

Add the corn kernels and melted butter to a bowl and let them have a party for about 5 minutes. Give it some flavor with a healthy pinch of both salt and pepper. Don't be shy; taste as you go. If the corn and butter mixture has gotten cold, microwave for about 1 minute or until it gets warm but not too hot. Pour in that glorious cheddar cheese and stir it all together until it's melted and creamy. Dish up that cheesy corn goodness immediately and get ready for compliments. It takes a fraction of the time our smokin' does, so enjoy!

COOKING TIME:
30 MINUTES
(1½ HOURS TOTAL TIME)

SERVES 8

MACARONI SALAD

Looking for a crowd-pleasing side dish that's perfect for your cookout? Look no further than this iconic macaroni salad recipe. It's all about striking the perfect balance of creamy, savory, and sweet flavors. Ditch the boring side dishes and impress your guests with this classic. It's sure to become a new favorite.

Kosher salt

1 pound elbow macaroni

2 celery ribs, finely diced

1 red bell pepper, seeded and finely diced

½ cup shredded carrots

½ cup finely diced red onion

1 cup mayonnaise

½ cup sour cream

¼ cup white vinegar

1 tablespoon white sugar

1 tablespoon yellow mustard

Freshly ground black pepper

Bring a large pot of salted water to a boil and cook the macaroni according to package directions. We want them just shy of al dente for the perfect texture. Once cooked, rinse them under cold water to stop the cooking process and add them to a large bowl. Next, add the celery, bell pepper, carrots, and onion to the semi-cooled noodles. Toss them together.

Now it's time to make that classic tangy dressing: In a separate bowl, whisk together the mayonnaise, sour cream, vinegar, sugar, mustard, and a pinch of pepper.

Pour three-fourths of the creamy dressing over the top of the cooled noodle mixture and toss everything together until evenly coated. Cover the bowl with plastic wrap and refrigerate the macaroni salad for at least 1 hour before serving. This allows all the flavors to meld and develop for a truly delicious result!

Right before you serve, add the rest of the dressing. The lukewarm pasta will have absorbed the dressing in the fridge, and this additional amount will coat the pasta and make it creamier when it's showtime.

TEXAS TWIST

Four Styles Collide for BBQ Bliss

BARBECUE
BARBECUE

WE'RE HITTING THE BARBEQUE TRAIL and heading straight into the heart of Texas. That's right, Texas, the Lone Star State, where barbeque isn't just food, it's a religion, a passion, and a way of life.

Now, let's get one thing straight: Texas barbeque is as diverse and expansive as the state itself. From the smoky brisket havens of Central Texas to the saucy pork palaces of East Texas and the fiery, mesquite-grilled meats of South Texas, the Lone Star State offers a barbeque experience like no other. This is a place where every pitmaster has a secret recipe, every wood has a story, and every bite is a taste of pure, unadulterated barbeque bliss.

We're about to embark on an epic, mouthwatering journey through the Texas barbeque scene. We've gone behind the scenes with legendary pitmasters, tasted our way through iconic dishes, and dived deep into the rich history and culture that make Texas barbeque truly special. We've laughed, we've learned, and, most importantly, we've feasted—because in Texas, barbeque isn't just about eating, it's about celebrating the art of slow-cooked, wood-smoked perfection.

This AC Texas BBQ chapter is your all-access pass to the smoky, saucy, and downright delicious world of Texas barbeque. We'll guide you through the dishes that embody the true AC spirit: where barbeque is more than just food, it's a celebration of flavor, community, and the pure joy of cooking over an open flame. Grab your cowboy boots and your appetite, because we're about to take you on a barbeque journey through Texas that you won't soon forget!

THE SPOTS

FRANKLIN BARBECUE

Get ready to join the legendary barbeque pilgrimage to Franklin Barbecue in Austin, y'all! Sure, the lines are long and the wait is real, but trust us, pitmaster Aaron Franklin's James Beard Award–winning briskets are worth every second. This place isn't just a barbeque joint; it's an institution that's been setting the gold standard for 'que since day one.

As for when to go, Franklin fires up the pits from Tuesday through Sunday, starting at 11 AM and serving until they sell out—which, let's be honest, is usually around 2 or 3 PM. You'll want to get there early to snag your favorites before they're gone! So, whether you're a seasoned barbeque aficionado or a curious foodie looking to taste the best of Austin, Franklin Barbecue offers a true barbeque experience that's as legendary as it is delicious. Get ready to join the line, soak in the smoky aroma, and feast like a true Texan.

LEROY AND LEWIS BARBECUE

Get ready to elevate your BBQ game with LeRoy and Lewis Barbecue. This barbeque joint makes modern, innovative 'que that's taking Austin's Garrison Park neighborhood by storm. At LeRoy and Lewis, they're flipping the script on traditional smoked meat classics. We're talking beef cheeks that melt in your mouth, halved avocados stuffed with barbacoa, vegan cauliflower burnt ends that'll make you question everything you thought you knew about barbeque, and maple-glazed bacon ribs that are pure bliss in every bite. And that's just the tip of the iceberg: They've got a whole slew of new options that'll keep you coming back for more.

VALENTINA'S TEX MEX BBQ

Y'all, let's take a trip down flavor lane with Valentina's, the Austin sensation that's been serving up mouthwatering barbeque with a Texas twist since 2013! Their weapon of choice is a mesquite wood–fired offset smoker. Let us tell you, it's a game-changer. The result? Fifteen-hour smoked brisket that's so lush and moist, it practically melts in your mouth. But here's where things get interesting: They're not just serving up brisket, they're wrapping it in homemade flour tortillas and lightly crisping them on the griddle. The result is a taco that's pure Texas heaven, with a campfire aroma that'll transport you straight to a Lone Star State cookout. Valentina's offers a dining experience that's as unique as it is delicious.

VERA'S BACKYARD BAR-B-QUE

Y'all, let's dive into a Brownsville, Texas, tradition that's been smokin' since 1955—we're talkin' about Vera's and their legendary barbacoa! Now, when we say old-school, we mean it—mesquite coals and a subterranean pit that's been passed down through generations. Trust us, it's a sight to behold. So, pro tip alert: Get there early and ask to check out the pits where the barbacoa is cooked. It's a behind-the-scenes glimpse that'll make your barbeque-loving heart skip a beat. Vera's offers a dining experience that's as authentic as it is delicious.

GATLIN'S BBQ

Gatlin's BBQ is a Houston gem! Pitmaster Greg Gatlin, a former defensive back at Rice University, knows a thing or two about strategy—and he's applying that same winning mindset to his barbeque empire. With a method that blends

hickory and oak in an indirect-heat pit, Greg's creations are nothing short of barbeque perfection.

While the brisket is smoky and satisfying, it's the pork ribs that steal the spotlight. Whether you prefer baby backs or St. Louis–cut, these ribs are tender, juicy, and seasoned to perfection. And let's not forget about the sausages. Gatlin's BBQ offers a dining experience that's as delicious as it is memorable.

VICTORIAN'S BBQ

If you find yourself near Waco, make the short drive out to Mart, Texas, for Victorian's BBQ, where pitmaster Joey Victorian is serving up some of the best smoke in the state. Joey earned national recognition as a standout contestant on season 2 of Netflix's *Barbecue Showdown*. But while the cameras put him on the map, his true passion has always been feeding people, and you can taste that joy in every bite.

At Victorian's, the vibe is small-town warm, the kind of place where locals and barbeque pilgrims rub elbows behind plates piled high with brisket, ribs, and Joey's signature sides. We consider ourselves lucky because we've been on the receiving end of his cooking, and trust us, it's every bit as good as you've heard.

COOKING TIME:
12 HOURS
(36 HOURS TOTAL TIME)

SERVES 12

DRY RUB BEEF BRISKET

Ever dream of replicating that legendary Texas BBQ brisket right at home? This recipe is your secret weapon! We'll guide you through the entire process, from seasoning to smoking to slicing, ensuring a tender, juicy, and incredibly flavorful result.

While Texas-style brisket has a reputation for difficulty, this recipe breaks it down into manageable steps. Even beginners can achieve restaurant-worthy results with our proven techniques and helpful tips.

1 (12-pound) whole packer brisket (point and flat together), untrimmed

12 ounces beef broth

Kosher salt

½ cup Put Me on Everything Rub (page 203)

Texas Mop Sauce (page 222)

Trim the fat: Remove most of the fat, leaving a thin layer (about ¼ inch) for flavor. Don't worry about precision here. For even cooking, you can separate the point from the flat. This allows for seasoning all sides of the flat and achieving a consistent smoke ring.

Injecting your meat with broth helps retain moisture during the long cook. We're trying to keep that meat moist. Broth does the job well; no need to add any spices or other flavors to the broth. We're not looking to overpower the meat's natural flavor.

Over a sink, inject the needle into the brisket parallel to the grain at 1-inch intervals. Apply a good amount of salt on the outside for maximum flavor penetration.

Before you start smoking, you gotta pay attention to the grain on this bad boy, folks. It's like knowin' your dance partner—we gotta cut that brisket perpendicular for the most tender slices. The grain might hide under that glorious bark later, so some folks like to mark it with a quick slice beforehand to indicate the direction of the grain. Once you got that figured out, it's time to smother this in our Put Me on Everything Rub. Don't be shy!

Store in your refrigerator for, ideally, 12 to 24 hours before you start smoking. If you're in a rush, 2 to 4 hours would work, but who is in a rush to make a smoked brisket?

It's important to keep it nice and chilled until cookin' time. Trust us, the colder it starts, the more smoke it soaks up. And for perfect results, grab yourself a remote digital thermometer. Stick that probe right in the thickest part of the meat, away from the heat source, and you'll be a grill master in no time!

Preheat your smoker to around 235°F. We want it to cook at 225°F, but the temperature will drop when you open the lid. Place the seasoned brisket on the smoker right above the water pan and add 2 cups of wood chips for smoky goodness. The low temperature and slow cook time are essential for achieving tenderness.

Here's the kicker: We ain't babysittin' this brisket! No moppin', bastin', or spritzin'. That just messes with the temp and weakens the bark. Just add another 4 ounces of wood chips every 30 minutes or so during those first 2 hours to keep the smoke flowin'. And don't let that water pan run dry, folks; gotta maintain a moist environment for this delicious journey. After 3 hours, if the top and bottom of the brisket ain't lookin' similar, then flip it over. Otherwise, just let that smoker work its magic. We ain't in the business of micromanaging good BBQ.

Brisket is gonna take its sweet time now. Watch that internal temp climb to around 150°F, but then hold on tight, 'cause we're entering the stall. That's right—the temp will act like it's stuck in molasses. It might even take 5 hours to budge just 5 degrees Fahrenheit! Don't you fret, though; this ain't no mistake. When the stall hits, we're gonna take that beautiful brisket and wrap it up tight in a double layer of heavy-duty foil, no air space allowed. Why? Because any air space lets precious

recipe continues

juices escape, and ain't nobody got time for that! This foil hug keeps the moisture locked in and prevents surface evaporation that messes with the temp. Wrap that brisket around 150°F and watch it power through the stall like a champ, shavin' hours off your cook time. Now, that's what we call smokin' smart!

Once the internal temperature reaches 195°F to 205°F, remove the brisket from the smoker and let it rest in a cooler for several hours to allow the juices to redistribute. If the foil is leaking, put it in a large pan and then into the cooler. Leave the meat probe in and wait until the meat drops down to 150°F.

Thinly slice the brisket against the grain for maximum tenderness. Brisket dries out quickly, so it's important to slice and serve it quickly. To carve this up like a pro: First, grab your sharpest knife and separate the flat from the point—think of it like isolatin' the dance floor. Trim off any extra fat that's just chillin'; we want all the good stuff.

Now comes the fun part: slicing. Take each muscle one at a time and go against the grain, nice and thin, about a quarter inch thick. You want those slices to hold their own, not turn to mush—but they should also still pull apart with a little love tap. If that first slice begins to break up, just make the slices a tad thicker.

We're sure that you cooked this perfectly, but let's say you didn't. That's OK—a full beef brisket is one of the hardest meats to get right, even for BBQ pros. To help give it some moisture, you can combine some Texas Mop Sauce with some dripping mixture. Just taste to make sure that combo is not too salty.

SQUIRT
OAK FARMS
Luxury
ICE CREAM
EXIT
BEVERAG
CALIFORNIA
RANGE
Miller Lite
879 LBG
PSN·49G
GGZ 189
568899
RAILWAY
PARTS AN
SERVICE
MEMBER
HOUSTON
THE PIT ROOM
NOTICE
OPEN

Coca-Cola
PAPPAS Bar-B-Q
Coca-Cola
PAPPAS Bar-B-Q
TEXAS
PAPPAS
SINCE 1967
PAPPAS

COOKING TIME: 30 MINUTES

SERVES 2

CEDDY'S BEEF BRISKET BURRITO

This is a flavor fiesta that'll have you jumpin' out of bed and doin' a jig before you can say "Good morning." Get ready for a symphony of textures and tastes that'll make your taste buds sing like a mariachi band at a fiesta. And we're going to use that amazing beef brisket we took all those hours smokin' and use it to start our day off right.

Vegetable oil

2 cups chopped Dry Rub Beef Brisket (page 126)

Texas Mop Sauce (page 222)

4 large eggs, beaten

Kosher salt

2 warm and toasty flour tortillas

8 ounces black beans, rinsed, drained, and warmed

8 ounces tater tots, cooked according to package instructions, warm

Shredded cheddar cheese

2 tablespoons tangy tomatillo sauce

Drizzle just enough oil to coat your griddle and toss on the brisket. Let it sizzle and crisp for about 3 minutes, flipping it like a champ until it's heated through. Once your brisket is lookin' good, toss it in a bowl with a few tablespoons of the Texas Mop Sauce. Make sure every piece gets a healthy dose of that smoky sweetness.

Next, we're going to cook our scrambled eggs. Add them to the griddle with a little more oil. Season slightly with salt. Cook, stirring occasionally, until the eggs are just set, about 3 minutes. Set aside.

Get your griddle nice and hot, then throw on those flour tortillas. Let them sizzle for about 10 seconds per side until they're nice and pliable.

Assemble your masterpiece: First, add your eggs to the tortilla. Then, top the eggs with that saucy, smoky brisket. Add a layer of those warm black beans and sprinkle on those crispy, salty tater tots. They're the surprise party in your mouth you never knew you needed. Top it all off with a nice layer of cheese. Because, let's be honest, everything is better with cheese. Drizzle that tangy tomatillo sauce on top for a flavor explosion that'll have you saying "Olé!"

Fold the bottom of the tortilla over the filling, then fold the sides in toward the center. Now roll it up tight like a breakfast burrito champion. Wrap in heavy-duty foil to keep it warm and secure. Make sure it's sealed tight; you don't want any of those explosive flavors escaping.

COOKING TIME: 20 MINUTES

SERVES 6

TEXAS-STYLE BRISKET QUESO

Yo, queso lovers—this one's for you. We're talkin' creamy, melty goodness inspired by the smoky flavors of the South but kicked up a notch with some secret AC fam tweaks. Now, purists might say all you need is cheese and tomatoes with a kick, but where's the fun in that? We're going to finish this with some beautiful Dry Rub Beef Brisket to make your taste buds sing.

1 (2-pound) block Velveeta, roughly chopped into 1-inch cubes

1 (10-ounce) can Ro-Tel diced tomatoes with green chiles

½ cup chopped fresh cilantro leaves

2 garlic cloves, minced

½ teaspoon ground cumin

½ teaspoon crushed red pepper flakes

¼ teaspoon dried oregano

¼ teaspoon grated lime zest, plus 2 teaspoons lime juice

¼ cup minced canned chipotle chiles en adobo (optional)

1 pound warmed Dry Rub Beef Brisket (page 126)

Tortilla chips

Throw that Velveeta, the Ro-Tel tomatoes with their juices, and ⅔ cup water into a medium saucepan over medium-low heat. Stir like a champ until the cheese is melted and everything is creamy and dreamy, about 5 minutes. This is the base of your queso kingdom.

Here's where the fun begins! Add your cilantro, garlic, cumin, red pepper flakes, oregano, lime zest, and lime juice to the pot. Stir it all together on low heat for about 5 minutes, letting those flavors get to know each other. Feeling like your queso needs a little more fire? Throw in some minced chipotle chiles en adobo. Just remember, with great heat comes great responsibility, so go slow and taste as you go.

Serve that queso up hot and bubbly in your favorite bowl topped with our beautiful Dry Rub Beef Brisket and some tortilla chips. Get ready for a flavor fiesta!

TIP: This queso will keep in the fridge for up to a week, but let's be real—it probably won't last that long once your crew gets hold of it!

Fritos
BRAND
The ORIGINAL

COOKING TIME: 15 MINUTES

SERVES 6

BRISKET FRITO PIE

Craving a taste of summer but short on time? Do you have some extra Dry Rub Beef Brisket in your fridge? Good—this Brisket Frito Pie is a fiesta in a bag, and it's here to save the day! It's like a portable party in your pantry, perfect for backyard cookouts, camping trips, or just a quick bite that'll have your taste buds doing the two-step.

6 (1-ounce) bags Fritos Corn Chips

4 cups warmed Dry Rub Beef Brisket (page 126)

2 cups shredded cheddar cheese

1 cup shredded lettuce

¼ cup diced fresh tomatoes, hothouse preferred

½ cup sour cream

¼ cup minced yellow onion

Texas Mop Sauce (page 222), for serving

Get rough with those Fritos! We don't want dust, but we don't want them totally intact either. Think of it like tenderizing a steak—gotta get those flavor channels open! Open up the bag nice and wide (maybe cut a little bit of the top off all around); this is your Frito Pie battleground.

Divide your Dry Rub Beef Brisket among your 6 open bags. Let those smoky, meaty flavors mingle with the Frito crunch. It's a match made in barbeque heaven!

Now comes the fun part: the fixin's. Top your brisket with some cheese and let it melt a tiny bit. Sprinkle on some lettuce for a cool contrast, then add a pop of color with diced tomatoes. Feeling fancy? Throw in some sour cream and finely minced onion.

Grab a plastic spoon (or go commando, we won't judge) and dive into this Frito Pie fiesta! Serve with a side of Texas Mop Sauce. It never hurts to give a little finger-lickin' dunk. It's perfect for satisfying your summer cravings on the go.

BBQ
S'mores
BBQ COMPANY
JUNE 23

THE
MANDALORIAN
SMOKERS

COOKING TIME:
5 MINUTES

SERVES 4

AC CHOPPED SANDWICH

Get ready to nuke your taste buds with this brisket bomb, a flavor explosion inspired by the pitmasters of Texas. This BBQ sandwich is a symphony of smokin'-good flavors that'll have you singin' its praises with every bite. And the best part is, it comes together incredibly fast, and you get to use up that huge, delicious Dry Rub Beef Brisket you cooked up.

Vegetable oil

4 golden brioche buns

1 pound Dry Rub Beef Brisket (page 126)

Texas Mop Sauce (page 222)

Apple Slaw (page 58), optional

Get your griddle nice and hot, then drizzle with enough oil to coat the bottom. Place those fluffy brioche buns cut-side down and let them toast to a golden crisp; about 10 seconds should do the trick. Take them off the heat and get ready for the main event.

Crisp up that brisket: Throw that Dry Rub Beef Brisket onto the griddle with another drizzle of oil. Let it sizzle and sizzle for about 3 minutes, flipping it constantly until it's nice and crispy and warmed all the way through.

Once your brisket is lookin' good, toss it in a bowl with our Texas Mop Sauce. Make sure every piece gets a healthy coating of that sweet and smoky goodness. Assemble your masterpiece: Place that saucy brisket on the toasted bottom bun and top with some Apple Slaw if you would like. You can pat yourself on the back because you're almost there.

Pop on the toasted top bun, and you've got yourself a brisket bomb ready to detonate in your mouth. Just remember, with this much flavor, you might need to share . . . maybe.

COOKING TIME: 6 HOURS (1 DAY TOTAL TIME)

MAKES 8 PATTIES

JALAPEÑO SAUSAGE PATTIES

Yo, grill masters and mistresses! This is our Jalapeño Sausage Patty—it'll leave your taste buds begging for more! We're talkin' smoky, cheesy goodness infused with a kick of jalapeño.

- **1½ pounds beef brisket**
- **1 pound brisket fat**
- **4 ounces pork butt**
- **3 tablespoons kosher salt**
- **1½ teaspoons freshly ground black pepper**
- **1½ teaspoons garlic powder**
- **1 teaspoon onion powder**
- **¼ teaspoon white sugar**
- **1 teaspoon chipotle powder**
- **1 teaspoon mild paprika**
- **2 teaspoons yellow mustard seed**
- **3 teaspoons crushed red pepper flakes**
- **4 tablespoons ice cold heavy cream**
- **1 small jalapeño, diced**
- **1 cup small cubes extra-sharp cheddar**

Clean off any silverskin, sinew, and arteries from your meat. Cut it into small strips or cubes. Then, throw that meat and fat in the freezer for an hour until it's nice and chilled. While the meat chills, get all your seasonings prepped: salt, pepper, garlic powder, onion powder, sugar, chipotle powder, paprika, mustard seed, and red pepper flakes.

Next, grind your chilled meat and fat on a medium plate. Toss all those spices, the cream, and the diced jalapeños into a mixer with the ground meat. Get in there and mix it all up until it becomes super tacky. Once that mix is nice and sticky, gently fold in the cheese, making sure all those cheesy bits get incorporated. Now form the mixture into 8 sausage patties and place them in an airtight container or on a sheet pan covered in plastic wrap. Refrigerate them overnight to allow the flavors to work their magic.

Preheat your griddle over medium-high heat and grill those patties about 5 minutes on each side to get some nice char. (Check for doneness with an instant-read thermometer; they should be cooked to 165°F.) That cheddar cheese is going to start melting and looking all beautiful. Serve them up with your favorite sides—we like Macaroni Salad (page 119) and Green Beans (page 76).

Dry Rub Beef Brisket, p. 126

Hot Guts Sausage, p. 146

Jalapeño Sausage Patties, p. 143

Texas Pork Spare Ribs, p. 147
Texas Mop Sauce, p. 222
Beef Short Ribs, p. 148

COOKING TIME: 2 HOURS

MAKES 8 LINKS

HOT GUTS SAUSAGE

Brisket might be the king of Texas BBQ, but there's another contender smokin' hot on its heels: the Hot Guts Sausage. It has bold flavors, juicy textures, and a rich history that goes back to the German and Czech settlers who brought their sausage-lovin' ways to the Lone Star State.

Made with a blend of beef and pork (some go pure beef, some pure pork; it's a choose-your-own-adventure kinda situation), Hot Guts are typically stuffed in natural casings and smoked low and slow over post oak wood. The result? A symphony of flavors that'll have your taste buds howling!

2 teaspoons cracked whole black peppercorns (keep them chunky) plus 2 teaspoons freshly ground black pepper

2 teaspoons kosher salt

2 teaspoons ground sage

2 teaspoons mild paprika

1 teaspoon cayenne pepper

1 teaspoon garlic powder

1 pound ground pork (80% lean)

1 pound ground beef chuck (80% lean)

2 tablespoons dry nonfat milk

4 feet of pork sausage casings

Mix your crushed black peppercorns, ground black pepper, salt, ground sage, paprika, cayenne pepper, and garlic powder in a large bowl. This is your flavor base!

Grind up your pork and beef chuck. Remember, we want about 20% fat content for maximum flavor and texture. If the mix is too lean, ask your butcher for some fat trimmings to add.

Combine that ground meat masterpiece with your spice mix, then add the dry nonfat milk and ⅓ cup very cold water. Get in there and mix it all up until it becomes sticky and awesome. Think of it like Play-Doh, but way tastier!

Time to break out your sausage stuffer and casings! Feed that mixture into the stuffer and crank out those perfect 6-inch links. Don't forget to prick any air bubbles with a needle before you twist and link them up.

Fire up your grill or smoker and set it to a steady 225°F (low and slow is the key!). Smoke those Hot Guts until they reach an internal temperature of 160°F. This will take about 90 minutes. The smoke time can vary depending on how much smoky goodness you desire.

You can enjoy your Hot Guts naked on a plate with crackers and hot sauce (the traditional Texas way), dressed up on a bun, or incorporated into a delicious dish. These Texas Hot Guts are guaranteed to have your taste buds singing the praises of the Lone Star State!

**COOKING TIME:
5 HOURS**

SERVES 6

TEXAS PORK SPARE RIBS

Alright, BBQ brethren! Today, we're ditchin' the sugary competition stuff and goin' full-on Central Texas with these amazing Texas Pork Spare Ribs. You'll swear that you are in barbeque heaven at Snow's or Franklin's after you eat these.

1 (2-pound) rack pork spare ribs, membrane removed and any excess fat trimmed

2 tablespoons coarsely ground black pepper

1 tablespoon kosher salt

Spray bottle filled with apple cider vinegar

Texas Mop Sauce (page 222)

Get your smoker fired up to 250°F and toss in some oak, mesquite, hickory, or pecan wood for that classic Texas smoke flavor. We're keeping it savory, Texas-style. So, we're gonna hit these ribs with a light coat of pepper and salt. Let them sit for 30 minutes to let those flavors meld.

Place those ribs on the smoker, bone side down. Depending on the size, this cook can take 4 to 5 hours. Keep an eye on them and spritz with some vinegar if they're lookin' a little dry. You should only spritz your ribs two to three times during the entire cook. We want those bones to peek through and the rack to bend, not break. The internal temp should be around 195°F when they're ready.

Once they're done smokin', let the ribs rest for 15 minutes to stop the cookin' process. Then, grab some heavy-duty foil. Lay down a generous strip of Texas Mop Sauce on the foil and spritz it with vinegar to dilute it. Then, place your ribs, meat-side down, on top of that saucy goodness.

Wrap those ribs up in the foil and let them sit for 1 to 2 hours in a cooler. This lets the flavors really come together and makes the meat tender. Finally, take those ribs out of the foil, pour the remaining sauce all over the meat side, and slice 'em up! Now go forth and conquer your BBQ cravings, friends. You've earned it!

COOKING TIME:
8½ HOURS

SERVES 8

BEEF SHORT RIBS

We're talkin' rich, decadent, melt-in-your-mouth goodness that'll have you singin' the praises of barbeque. Now, I know what you're thinkin': "Guys, these sound a little too fancy for my backyard smoker." But fear not! These bad boys are surprisingly easy to cook, even for the grilling novice; and we're going to serve them with our delectable Texas Mop Sauce.

1 (3- to 5-pound) rack beef short ribs

Crystal Hot Sauce

¼ cup coarsely ground black pepper

¼ cup kosher salt

Spray bottle filled with water

Texas Mop Sauce (page 222)

Get that smoker up to 285°F and make sure the water pan is full. We want a steady low and slow cook. Beef ribs are usually pretty clean, but if you see any excess fat, trim it away. We want the good stuff, not the greasy stuff.

Brush on a light layer of hot sauce. This is where the magic happens. Now for the star of the show: Mix together your pepper and salt and apply a generous amount to your short ribs. Remember, these ribs are rich, so don't be shy.

Place those ribs meat side up on the smoker. We want that smoky goodness to penetrate deep into the meat. Cook for about 8 hours, low and slow. During the last few hours, spritz those ribs pretty frequently (about every 20 minutes) to keep them moist and to prevent burning.

How do you know they're done? When a toothpick easily slides between the membranes and the meat feels like melted butter, you've hit gold (or should I say, smoky goodness!). Aim for an internal temp of 205°F for good measure.

Let those ribs rest for at least 30 minutes before diggin' in. This lets the juices redistribute for maximum flavortown. There you have it, folks! A guaranteed crowd-pleaser that'll leave everyone begging for more. Serve with a side of the amazing Texas Mop Sauce.

OTHER AMERICAN FAVORITES

Fire up those grills and get ready to embark on a cross-country BBQ road trip. We're leaving no stone unturned as we explore the mouthwatering American barbeque favorites that go beyond the usual suspects. From coast to coast, we're uncovering BBQ gems that'll have you saying, "Y'all, this is some next-level stuff!"

Grab your grilling gear and your appetite, because this chapter is a culinary journey you won't want to miss. From smoky chicken and spicy ribs to buttery lobster and fresh salmon, we're serving up BBQ favorites from all across the nation. Get ready to cook, feast, and celebrate the diverse and delicious world of American barbeque—AC Barbeque style!

COOKING TIME: 45 MINUTES

SERVES 8

SMOKED CHICKEN
WITH ALABAMA WHITE SAUCE

We're all about the legendary white BBQ sauce. It's a Decatur, Alabama, original, a white masterpiece that elevates our juicy smoked chicken to new heights. Now, we know some folks raise an eyebrow at white sauce on barbeque, but trust us, this ain't no sweet, sticky mess. It's a tangy, vinegar-based dream that complements chicken like no other. This sauce is magic on chicken, but don't be afraid to use it in coleslaw or even on pulled pork.

Kosher salt

2 (4-pound) chickens, cut into quarters

Alabama White BBQ Sauce (page 223)

Salt your chickens well. Crank up your smoker or get your grill ready for some two-zone indirect cooking. We're looking for a steady 325°F on the indirect side. Place those chicken quarters skin side up on the indirect heat. If you're using a smoker, add a handful of wood chips or chunks for that smoky goodness (don't overdo it, though).

These birds won't cook all at once, so keep an eye on them. Use a probe to check the internal temp in the thickest part of each piece (don't touch the bone!). Wings cook faster, so put them on later and take them off earlier. Once everything hits around 155°F, flip those birds and get that skin nice and crispy on the hot side. When they reach 165°F, it's time for the sauce!

Baste those chickens generously on all sides with some of your Alabama white sauce. Plate up those beauties, grab some extra sauce for dippin', and get ready for a smoky, creamy, and unforgettable chicken experience. This is next-level deliciousness. Now get cookin'!

COOKING TIME: 3½ HOURS (AT LEAST 4 HOURS TOTAL TIME)

SERVES 4

JERK RIBS

Get ready for an explosion of flavor that'll have your taste buds doin' the reggae! This is a jerk marinade—a symphony of heat, allspice, and thyme with a hint of sweetness from rum. It's so versatile, you can slap it on chicken, pork tenderloin, or even tofu (yeah, you heard that right!). But today, we're focusin' on ribs—baby back ribs, to be exact.

- **1 bunch scallions, trimmed and roughly chopped**
- **½ small yellow onion, roughly chopped**
- **4 garlic cloves**
- **4 habanero peppers, stemmed and seeded**
- **Kosher salt**
- **2 tablespoons dried thyme**
- **2 tablespoons ground allspice**
- **1 tablespoon garlic powder**
- **1 teaspoon chipotle powder**
- **½ teaspoon chili powder**
- **1 tablespoon packed dark brown sugar**
- **Freshly ground black pepper**
- **¼ cup soy sauce**
- **¼ cup dark rum**
- **2 racks baby back ribs, membrane removed**

Grab the scallions, onion, garlic, and habanero peppers. Throw them in a food processor with a pinch of salt and hit pulse for a nice mince.

Add the thyme, allspice, garlic powder, chipotle powder, chili powder, brown sugar, a few hits of black pepper, and the soy sauce to that food processor party. Blend it up for 20 seconds, then pulse in that dark rum for good measure. Feeling the marinade's a little thick? Add up to ¼ cup of water to thin it out. Don't forget to refrigerate this fiery concoction for at least 30 minutes (or until you're ready to get cookin'). It'll keep in the fridge for a few days if you get some leftover marinade magic.

When you are ready to cook, heat your smoker or oven to 300°F. Time to get those baby back ribs ready for their transformation. Season the ribs generously with salt and pepper, then lay each rack of ribs on a big sheet of aluminum foil. Now comes the fun part: Slather them in that jerk marinade! Wrap those ribs up tight in the foil like a delicious

recipe continues

present and place them on a sheet pan in the oven or right on the grates of your smoker. Let them slow roast for 90 minutes, letting the flavors meld and the meat get nice and tender.

After their steamy slumber, take those ribs out of the oven and carefully unwrap them. Time to crank up the flavor another notch! Anoint those ribs with even more jerk marinade, then toss them back in the oven or smoker, uncovered, for another 90 minutes. This will create a beautiful crust and make the meat beautifully tender.

Let those ribs rest for a few minutes to redistribute all that juicy goodness. Then, slice 'em up and serve them on a warm platter. Island fire awaits, my friends! Dig in and enjoy!

COOKING TIME:
30 MINUTES

SERVES 2

MAINE LOBSTER
WITH COWBOY BUTTER SAUCE

Ahoy there, seafood lovers! We're here to challenge a fishy tale: Boiled lobster ain't the only way to sail the seas of flavor. We're talkin' grilled lobster, baby—a revelation for any landlocked buccaneer.

Sure, grillin' gives it a bit more chew than boilin', but that just means a smidge more effort for a treasure trove of taste. The dry heat intensifies the lobster's natural sweetness, unlike boilin', which can leave it a tad bland. Plus, you get a hint of smoky goodness that's impossible to achieve indoors, like a campfire kiss on your taste buds.

We're also here to add a little somethin' special to this smoked lobster with this lip-smackin' cowboy butter recipe. It's a compound butter that's perfect for smotherin' grilled steak, chicken, shrimp, veggies, you name it!

8 tablespoons (1 stick) unsalted butter

4 garlic cloves, minced

1 tablespoon Dijon mustard

Grated zest and juice of ½ lemon, plus 4 lemon wedges for serving

1 tablespoon chopped fresh flat-leaf parsley

1 teaspoon chopped fresh chives

1 teaspoon chopped fresh thyme

1 teaspoon paprika

1 teaspoon cayenne pepper

½ teaspoon crushed red pepper flakes

Kosher salt

Freshly ground black pepper

2 (1½- to 2-pound) whole live Maine lobsters

In a pan, gently melt the butter. Stir in the garlic, mustard, lemon zest and juice, parsley, chives, thyme, paprika, cayenne pepper, red pepper flakes, a pinch of salt, and a pinch of black pepper until well combined. Set aside two-thirds of the butter for serving and place the rest next to your grill.

First, we must handle our lobsters with respect. We recommend plunging a knife straight down into the head of each lobster. Place the tip of a sharp chef's knife behind the lobster's eyes, right below where the claws meet the body and halfway to the first joint. Swiftly plunge the knife down through the head. The legs will continue to move a bit afterward, but the lobster is in fact dead.

Set your grill to direct heat, aiming for a medium-hot zone around 400°F. It's gonna get hot in here! Place those lobster halves shell-side down on the hot grill. The shell acts like a natural shield, so nestle it

recipe continues

between the grates to prevent rolling. Those big claws might need some wrangling, so feel free to maneuver them or place the halves side-by-side for stability.

Brush that luscious cowboy butter all over the lobster meat. Close the lid for a few minutes, then open it up and baste again for good measure. Your lobster is ready to devour when the thickest part of the tail hits 145°F and turns from translucent to a beautiful pearly white. Cooking them should take about 8 minutes total. Give it one last loving baste before taking it off the heat.

Time to unleash the deliciousness! Crack open those claws (carefully!) with a cracker, rolling pin, or whatever tool feels right. Serve it with the reserved butter for dipping, and a squeeze of lemon for those who like a bit of zing.

COOKING TIME:
25 MINUTES

SERVES 4

NORTHWEST GRILLED SALMON

Dive into the flavors of the Pacific Northwest right in your backyard with our Northwest Grilled Salmon recipe. Inspired by the region's rich culinary heritage, this dish captures the essence of the Northwest's pristine waters and lush landscapes, delivering a taste sensation that's both fresh and flavorful.

In just twenty-five minutes, you'll be serving up a mouthwatering meal that's perfect for sharing with family and friends. Start with a beautiful piece of salmon, preferably wild-caught to honor the Northwest's commitment to sustainable fishing practices.

2 pounds salmon fillets, skin on

4 tablespoons (½ stick) salted butter

¼ cup packed light brown sugar

2 tablespoons soy sauce

1 tablespoon Worcestershire sauce

½ teaspoon garlic powder

Preheat a grill to medium high.

Grab a large sheet of heavy-duty aluminum foil and lay it flat. Gently place your salmon on top, skin side down. Fold up the edges to create a little foil boat to catch all those delicious juices.

Dot the top of your salmon with little pats of butter. Then, sprinkle the brown sugar evenly for a touch of sweetness. Finally, drizzle with the soy sauce, Worcestershire sauce, and garlic powder. Carefully fold up the long sides of the foil, then crimp the ends to create a tight seal. We want all those yummy juices to stay inside and mingle with the salmon.

Place your foil packet on the grill. Let it cook for 15 to 20 minutes, depending on your grill's heat. The packet will puff up a bit when it's done—that's your cue to check on the salmon, because it should be ready.

COOKING TIME:
30 MINUTES

SERVES 4

GRILLED OYSTERS

We're setting sail on a flavor adventure with these beauties of the sea: grilled oysters! Get ready for plump, juicy oysters bathed in a bubbling, lip-smacking compound butter. They cook up fast on a hot grill, so fire it up. The key is keeping them on the heat for just a few minutes, ensuring they stay perfectly plump and bursting with flavor.

For a truly stress-free experience, delegate the shucking to a willing first mate. But if you're flying solo, no worries! Just open those oysters carefully beforehand. Here's the trick: Handle them with care to avoid spilling the precious liquor inside. That magical elixir combines with the melted butter for a flavor explosion that's truly unforgettable.

16 tablespoons (2 sticks) salted butter

3 tablespoons Crystal Hot Sauce, plus more for serving

1 small garlic clove, smashed

1 lemon, zested and cut into wedges for serving

1 anchovy

24 oysters

Toss the butter, hot sauce, garlic, lemon zest, and anchovy into a food processor and blitz it up until there are no streaks of hot sauce in sight. You want a beautiful, pale pink masterpiece. If you don't have a food processor, no problem—just beat it all together with a spoon until it's nice and smooth. Scrape it into a bowl and let it chill in the fridge.

Scrub those oysters clean in a large bowl to remove any uninvited guests (think sand or grit). Once they're sparkling clean, rinse them well and pop them in the fridge until it's grilling time!

For the brave souls who dare to shuck, here's a quick lesson: Grab an oyster with a folded dish towel, holding it shell side down with the hinge facing you. Take your oyster knife and carefully insert the tip into the hinge, then give it a twist to crack it open. Make sure your knife is clean and free of any shell fragments. Use it to detach the top shell and then slide it under the oyster meat to separate it from the bottom shell. Repeat with all your oysters and discard any that are already open or smell a bit off.

Get that grill roaring, whether it's charcoal or gas. We want a high heat. Crumple up a sheet of aluminum foil to create little cradles for your oysters. This will prevent them from tipping over and spilling their delicious juices.

Place your oysters on the foil and dollop each one with about ½ teaspoon of that glorious compound butter. For the larger oysters, feel free to be a bit more generous, but go easy on the smaller ones.

The goal is to coat them in flavor, not drown them! Close the lid and let them cook for 3 minutes, until the butter and oyster juices are bubbling merrily and the oysters are still nice and plump.

Carefully use tongs to transfer those beauties to a platter lined with another piece of foil (this keeps the shells upright). Serve them immediately with the lemon wedges and a bottle of hot sauce for an extra flavor punch, and get ready for a taste of the sea that will have you saying "Arr!" with delight!

COOKING TIME:
30 MINUTES

SERVES 6

ELOTE SALAD WITH CRACKLIN'S

Calling all cob enthusiasts! We all love elote, but sometimes you just want those delicious corn kernels without the messy cobs. Well, move over, boring salads, because elote salad is here to add a fiesta to your taste buds! This recipe is super easy to whip up, taking just about thirty minutes from start to finish.

½ cup mayonnaise

Juice of 1 lime

½ teaspoon chili powder

¼ teaspoon smoked paprika

Crystal Hot Sauce

Vegetable oil

6 ears fresh corn, in their husks

½ cup crumbled Cotija cheese

½ cup coarsely chopped fresh cilantro leaves

3 scallions, sliced

Cracklin's (page 168)

In a bowl, whisk together the mayonnaise, lime juice, chili powder, paprika, and a few dashes of hot sauce. This is your flavorful base, so give it a taste and adjust the seasonings to your liking. Then, pop it in the fridge to chill.

Fire up your grill to medium heat and give the grates a light oil coating. Grill your corn away from the direct heat for 15 to 20 minutes. Let the ears cool down a bit so you can handle them easily. Now for the fun part! Shuck those cobs and let them cool completely.

With a sharp knife, cut those kernels off the cobs. In a large bowl, combine the corn, Cotija cheese, cilantro, and scallions. Finally, fold in that chilled chile-lime mayonnaise and get ready for that dynamite seasoning! Serve in your prettiest bowl with some fire cracklin's on top.

SNACKS, DESSERTS & DRINKS

Alright, y'all, it's time to give your taste buds a little something extra with our ultimate guide to BBQ snacks, desserts, and drinks. We all know that BBQ isn't just about the main event: It's also about those irresistible bites, sweet treats, and drinks that keep us coming back for more. So, whether you're looking to kick off your BBQ feast with some finger-lickin'-good snacks, satisfy your sweet tooth with a decadent dessert, or pack a punch and elevate your BBQ experience, we've got you covered from start to finish.

Whether you're snacking on cracklin's or indulging in a slice of sweet potato pie, this chapter is your go-to guide for all things BBQ snacks and desserts. Raise a glass and let's cheer to the perfect BBQ companion: drinks that pack a punch and elevate your BBQ experience. Nothing pairs better with smoky meats than the perfect snack, dessert, or drink. Cheers to flavor, fun, and unforgettable BBQ moments.

CGD
MASTER-TOUCH

**COOKING TIME:
5 HOURS**

SERVES 6

CRACKLIN'S

We all know that satisfying crunch you crave. Well, move over potato chips, because homemade cracklin's are here to steal the show! Forget the store-bought stuff—those greasy, flavorless shadows of a snack. This recipe is all about homemade cracklin's that are ridiculously crispy, bursting with flavor, and insanely addictive. We're talking "can't-put-the-bag-down" good. Intrigued? Let's get cracklin' (see what we did there?)!

1 pound pork skins
Kosher salt
Memphis Dry Rub (page 216)
Hot sauce (optional)

If there are any stray hairs on the skins, use a lighter to carefully singe them off. Then, give the skins a good wipe-down. They can be tough to cut, so pop them in the freezer for 30 to 45 minutes to firm up.

Once the skins are nice and stiff, grab a sharp knife and cut them into 1-inch-wide strips. Hold off on cutting squares yet or they might fall through the grill grates. In a large pot, cover the skins with water and bring it to a boil. Let them simmer for 30 minutes with the lid on. This helps render out some fat and softens those tough fibers. Drain the water and discard the rendered fat.

Seasoning savvy: Now comes the fun part! Sprinkle the wet skins generously with salt, just like you would popcorn. Then, dust them with our magical Memphis Dry Rub. Craving some heat? Feel free to add your favorite hot sauce too!

By now, the skins should be nice and puffy. Place them fat-side down on your smoker or grill, using indirect heat, at 225°F for an hour. Then, crank up the heat to 400°F to render out even more fat for 45 minutes or until they're golden brown and delicious (but not burnt!).

Just like with bacon, you can take your cracklin's to the next level of crispiness or enjoy them while they're still a bit moist and juicy. The choice is yours! Experiment and find your perfect texture.

Spread some paper towels on a large sheet pan on your counter and dump on those cracklin's. There should be minimal grease to be soaked up. Let them cool for at least 15 minutes, then cut those strips into squares if that's your preference.

Give them a try and adjust the seasonings to your liking. Want more flavor? Add a dash of salt, Memphis Dry Rub, or hot sauce.

These gold nuggets are best enjoyed fresh, but you can store them in the refrigerator in zip-top bags for a week or two. Just be warned that they tend to lose their magic after a while. To reheat, cook in your oven or grill at 200°F for 10 to 15 minutes. Stay away from the microwave—they might explode!

COOKING TIME: 10 MINUTES

MAKES 3 CUPS

PIMENTO CHEESE

Pimento cheese. It's a taste of the South. This creamy, cheesy spread is a staple across the Bible Belt, enjoyed on sandwiches or crackers or straight out of the tub (no judgment). This recipe is a classic: simple yet divine. A perfect blend of sharp cheddar, sweet pimentos, and rich mayonnaise. So, whether you're a Southerner by birth or just by taste, this pimento cheese is sure to become a new favorite.

- 2 cups grated extra-sharp cheddar cheese
- 1 cup softened cream cheese
- ½ cup mayonnaise
- 1 (4-ounce) jar pimentos, drained and diced
- ¼ teaspoon cayenne pepper
- ¼ teaspoon onion powder
- Kosher salt
- Freshly ground black pepper

In a large mixing bowl, create a cheesy landscape with your freshly grated cheddar. Add the softened cream cheese, mayonnaise, diced pimentos, cayenne pepper, onion powder, and a dash of salt and pepper to the cheddar. Now, gently fold everything together with a spatula until you have a smooth, spreadable pimento cheese masterpiece. Serve with veggies, crackers, or anything else you can think of.

COOKING TIME: 45 MINUTES

MAKES 24 EGGS

PAPRIKA DEVILED EGGS

Calling all deviled egg devotees! Get ready to elevate your expectations with our Paprika Deviled Eggs—a classic recipe with a twist that's both sophisticated and addictively delicious. We're talking about the perfect marriage of creamy, savory goodness with a touch of smoky magic. A hint of hot smoked paprika adds a layer of depth and intrigue that will tantalize your taste buds. Get that smoky taste without opening your smoker!

1 dozen large eggs

1 garlic clove

Kosher salt

½ cup mayonnaise

2 tablespoons tomato paste

2 teaspoons white vinegar

Freshly ground black pepper

¼ teaspoon smoked paprika, plus more for serving

We're all about achieving that creamy yolk, so follow our foolproof boiling method. Place the eggs in a pot, cover them with cold water, and bring them to a full boil. Let them cook for 1 minute, then turn off the heat and cover the pan. Let the eggs sit for 12 minutes before putting them directly in an ice bath.

Once the eggs are cool enough to handle, peel them carefully and cut them in half lengthwise. Scoop out the yolks and place them in a bowl, saving the egg whites on a platter for later.

Using a knife, mince the garlic with a pinch of salt to create a flavorful paste. You can use a spoon to press down on the garlic and salt to combine after you've minced. Add this paste to the yolks and mash everything together with a fork.

Now, here comes the fun part! Add the mayonnaise, tomato paste, vinegar, a pinch of pepper, and the paprika to the yolk mixture. Mash everything together until it's smooth and creamy. Taste and adjust the seasonings to your liking—more vinegar for a tang, more paprika for a smokier experience.

Spoon the creamy yolk mixture back into the egg white halves. Dust the tops with a sprinkle of paprika for an extra touch of smoky sophistication. There you have it! Paprika Deviled Eggs that are sure to impress your guests.

Fried Cheese Curds, p. 175

Fried Green Tomatoes, p. 176

Fried pickles, p. 177

COOKING TIME: 25 MINUTES

SERVES 6

FRIED CHEESE CURDS

These ain't your average, flavorless cheese curds. We're talking about ridiculously delicious Fried Cheese Curds that will have you reaching for handful after handful. They're the perfect party starter, game day companion, or anytime snack you crave. And the best part? They're incredibly easy to make. Just a few pantry staples are all you need to create this appetizer magic. Ready to unlock the cheesy potential of these little nuggets of deliciousness? Let's get frying!

Vegetable oil

¾ cup whole buttermilk

¾ cup all-purpose flour

1 teaspoon garlic salt

½ teaspoon cayenne pepper

½ teaspoon baking soda

1 large egg

1 pound white cheddar cheese curds

Get 3 inches of oil nice and hot (375°F) using a thermometer in a large Dutch oven.

In a bowl, whisk together the buttermilk, flour, garlic salt, cayenne pepper, baking soda, and egg until you have a smooth batter. Gently coat a few cheese curds at a time in the batter, making sure they're evenly covered. Carefully drop the battered curds into the hot oil and fry for just a few seconds, until they're golden brown and irresistible. Transfer the fried curds to a plate lined with paper towels to drain any excess oil.

These cheese curds are best served hot and fresh, so dig in and enjoy that melty, crispy goodness!

COOKING TIME:
30 MINUTES

SERVES 4

FRIED GREEN TOMATOES

Fried green tomatoes: a dish that whispers of summertime on the porch swing, sweet tea in hand. But these aren't your average, greasy fried tomatoes. These are golden-fried masterpieces with a hint of Southern charm. A sprinkle of Cajun seasoning adds a touch of smoky spice that elevates this dish to a whole new level.

3 medium green tomatoes
Kosher salt
1 cup all-purpose flour
1 tablespoon Cajun seasoning
½ cup whole buttermilk
1 large egg
⅓ cup fine white cornmeal
½ cup panko breadcrumbs
Canola oil

Slice your unpeeled tomatoes into ½-inch-thick rounds, then sprinkle them with a generous pinch of salt. Let them rest for 5 minutes, allowing the salt to draw out any excess moisture.

Set up your assembly line—three shallow bowls will do the trick. In the first, whisk together the flour and Cajun seasoning. In the second, combine the buttermilk and egg. In the third, mix the cornmeal and breadcrumbs.

Heat an inch of oil over medium heat in a skillet. Now for the fun part! Dredge each tomato slice in the flour mixture, then give it a dunk in the buttermilk-egg bath, and finally coat it generously in the cornmeal-breadcrumb mixture.

Carefully add half of the breaded tomatoes to the hot oil and fry for 3 to 5 minutes per side, until they're a beautiful golden brown. Transfer your fried green tomatoes to a plate lined with paper towels to drain any excess oil. Repeat with the remaining tomatoes.

These beauties are perfect on their own, but feel free to add a dollop of hot sauce for an extra kick of flavor. These fried green tomatoes are sure to transport you to the heart of the South.

COOKING TIME: 15 MINUTES

SERVES 4

FRIED PICKLES

Forget the floppy, flavorless pickles from the jar. We're talking about fried pickles—a symphony of crispy perfection with a tangy pickle heart. These little guys are the ideal appetizer or side dish, guaranteed to tantalize your taste buds and leave you reaching for more. Pair these with our Dill Pickle Potato Chips with Homemade Sour Cream Onion Dip for your next cookout and put that drained pickle juice to work!

Vegetable oil

½ cup all-purpose flour

1 teaspoon St. Louis Dry Rub (page 213)

Kosher salt

Freshly ground black pepper

1 tablespoon hot sauce

16 ounces dill pickles, sliced, drained, and dried (reserve your pickle brine for Dill Pickle Potato Chips with Homemade Sour Cream Onion Dip, page 179)

Ketchup, for serving

Add at least 2 inches of oil to your Dutch oven and get it up to 375°F.

While your oil is heating up, in a shallow bowl, whisk together the flour, St. Louis Dry Rub, a pinch of salt, a few cracks of pepper, and the hot sauce. Add cold water a little bit at a time and whisk until you have a smooth batter. You should use around ½ cup of water.

Working in batches, toss the dried pickle slices in the batter to coat them evenly. Let any excess drip off before carefully dropping the battered pickles into the hot oil and frying for 1 to 2 minutes, until they're golden brown and irresistible. Transfer the fried pickles to a paper towel–lined plate to drain any excess oil.

Serve your fried pickles with ketchup for dipping or enjoy them on their own!

COOKING TIME:
1½ HOURS
(AT LEAST 2½ HOURS TOTAL TIME)

SERVES 8

DILL PICKLE POTATO CHIPS

WITH HOMEMADE SOUR CREAM ONION DIP

Calling all chip connoisseurs! Ditch the greasy, store-bought bags and elevate your snacking game with these Dill Pickle Potato Chips with Homemade Sour Cream Onion Dip. We're talking about crispy perfection with a tangy, puckery punch thanks to a secret weapon: pickle brine. And forget the artificial flavors and mystery ingredients of store-bought onion dip. We're bringing you a recipe for homemade onion dip that's so easy and so delicious, you'll never go back to the powdered stuff. Serve these at your cookout with Fried Pickles (page 177).

HOMEMADE SOUR CREAM ONION DIP

⅓ cup vegetable oil

1 yellow onion, minced

Kosher salt

½ teaspoon white sugar

1 cup sour cream

DILL PICKLE POTATO CHIPS

2 russet potatoes, thinly sliced

2 cups pickle brine

2 tablespoons extra-virgin olive oil

1 tablespoon chopped fresh dill leaves, plus more for garnish

1 teaspoon garlic powder

½ teaspoon onion powder

½ teaspoon crushed red pepper flakes

Kosher salt

Freshly ground black pepper

First, we're going to make that caramelized magic dip: Heat the vegetable oil in a skillet over medium-high heat. Add the onions, a pinch of salt, and the sugar. Heat the onions, stirring occasionally, for about 10 minutes. They should become beautifully golden brown.

Pour the caramelized onions and oil into a fine-mesh strainer. Let the oil drain into a container (you can save it for another use) and scrape the softened onions into a bowl. Stir the sour cream into the caramelized onions. Cover the bowl and refrigerate while you prepare the dill pickle chips. The flavors will continue to develop, so if you want to make this the night before the cookout, that's even more ideal.

recipe continues

Let's make our dill pickle chips: Place your thinly sliced potatoes in a large bowl and cover them completely with pickle brine. Let them soak for at least 1 hour or up to 3 hours in the fridge for maximum pickle flavor infusion.

Preheat your oven to 400°F. Once the potatoes are done marinating, drain them and pat them completely dry. In a large bowl, toss the potatoes with the extra-virgin olive oil, dill, garlic powder, onion powder, and red pepper flakes. Season generously with salt and pepper.

Spread the potatoes out in a single layer on a large baking sheet, making sure none are overlapping. This ensures even crisping. Bake for 40 minutes, flipping the chips halfway through, until they're tender on the inside and irresistibly crisp and golden brown on the outside.

Garnish your golden chips with an extra sprinkle of fresh dill for a pop of color and flavor. Serve with your homemade sour cream onion dip. Welcome—you have reached the next level!

COOKING TIME:
1 HOUR

SERVES 8

PEACH COBBLER
WITH VANILLA BEAN ICE CREAM

Let's get down to business! This ain't just your grandma's cobbler: It's a whole lotta hot damn. This is the peach cobbler that's gonna make your taste buds do a two-step.

FOR THE PEACHES

5 peaches, peeled, cored, and sliced (about 4 cups)

¾ cup white sugar

Sea salt

FOR THE COBBLER

6 tablespoons unsalted butter

1 cup all-purpose flour

1 cup white sugar

2 teaspoons baking powder

¼ teaspoon sea salt

¾ cup milk

Ground cinnamon

Vanilla bean ice cream

Grab those fresh peaches and toss 'em in a saucepan with the sugar and a pinch of sea salt. Stir it up! Cook 'em on medium heat for a hot minute, just until that sugar dissolves and those peachy juices start flowing. Take the pan off the heat and let it chill on your kitchen counter.

Now, let's get that oven heated up to a sizzling 350°F. Throw that butter into your 9 x 13-inch baking dish and pop it in the oven to melt that golden goodness.

While that butter's melting away, mix up your flour, sugar, baking powder, and sea salt in a big bowl. Whisk in the milk until it's all combined and creamy. Once the butter's all melty, pour that batter over it, making sure it's nice and even. Time for those peaches! Spoon 'em and their juice all over that batter. Don't skimp on the cinnamon—sprinkle it generously over the top. Bake that beauty for about 40 minutes, until it's golden and bubbling.

Serve it up warm with a scoop of vanilla bean ice cream. Wipe the flavor off your face, 'cause this peach cobbler is a whole lotta hot goodness!

COOKING TIME: 45 MINUTES

SERVES 10

PUT ME ON EVERYTHING CARAMEL POPCORN

Let's take popcorn to the next level with this Put Me on Everything Caramel Popcorn masterpiece! This movie-night snack has a whole lotta hot flavor in every bite.

FOR THE CARAMEL POPCORN

3 quarts popped unsalted popcorn

3/4 cup packed dark brown sugar

6 tablespoons unsalted butter

3 tablespoons corn syrup

3/4 teaspoon fine sea salt

3/4 teaspoon vanilla extract

1 1/2 teaspoons baking soda

FOR THE PUT ME ON EVERYTHING POPCORN

3/4 cup Put Me on Everything Rub (page 203)

1/2 teaspoon fine sea salt

3 quarts popped unsalted popcorn

3 tablespoons unsalted butter, melted, plus more if needed

Heat that oven to a cozy 250°F and line 2 rimmed baking sheets with parchment paper. Let's get this party started!

First, let's make the caramel popcorn: Place your popcorn in a mega-sized mixing bowl. In a pot, bring the brown sugar, butter, and corn syrup to a foamy boil. Cook, stirring, until everything's melted and gooey, 2 to 3 minutes. Remove from the heat and stir in that sea salt and vanilla. Next, add the baking soda. Pour over your popcorn and mix it up real good. Spread it out on your baking sheets, pop it in the oven, and bake until it's crisp. Give it a mix halfway through. Test a piece—if it's crispy, it's ready to rock! Let it cool.

While that caramel magic is baking, whisk the Put Me on Everything Rub with the sea salt in a small bowl. Place your popcorn in a large mixing bowl, pour that melted butter over it, and toss it like you mean it. Sprinkle on the Put Me on Everything mix and give it another good toss. If it looks a tad dry, add more butter. Spread that goodness onto your second baking sheet. Bake it up until it's dry and delightful, tossing it halfway through. Let it cool. It's worth the wait!

Combine that caramel and Put Me on Everything popcorn and dig in! Pack it up in tins, jars, or bags, and you've got yourself the ultimate snack.

**COOKING TIME:
2 HOURS**

**MAKES 1
FINGER-LICKIN' PIE**

ANTHONY'S SWEET POTATO PIE

Hey, fam—let's dive into a slice of Southern comfort with this sweet potato pie! This ain't your grandma's recipe: It's Anthony's favorite, so bake one up and chow down.

3 medium sweet potatoes, peeled

5 tablespoons unsalted butter, at room temperature

¾ cup white sugar

1¼ teaspoons freshly ground nutmeg

1 large egg

½ teaspoon vanilla extract

2¼ teaspoons baking powder

3 tablespoons evaporated milk

1 frozen pie crust

Get those sweet potatoes in a big saucepan, cover 'em with water, and bring 'em to a boil. Reduce the heat and let 'em simmer until they're super tender, about 45 minutes. Drain 'em well. Mash those sweet potatoes up in a bowl. You should end up with about 2¾ cups of mashed potato goodness.

Preheat that oven to 350°F. Add that butter to your hot mashed potatoes and mash it all up until it's smooth like silk. Mix in that sugar, nutmeg, egg, and vanilla. In another bowl, combine the baking powder with your evaporated milk and blend it in. Add your wet ingredients to your potato mixture and whisk it all together until it's velvety smooth.

Pile that deliciousness into your pie crust, spreading it out nice and even to the edges. Bake that pie until it's set and has a nice light brown top, about 1 hour. Let it cool to room temp before you dig in.

COOKING TIME: 15 MINUTES

SERVES 5

DEEP-FRIED UNCRUSTABLES

Get ready to elevate your snack game with these Deep-Fried Uncrustables! We're taking your classic PB&J and turning it into hand pies that'll have everyone jumping for joy!

½ cup white sugar
1 tablespoon ground cinnamon
Canola oil
10 Uncrustables, unwrapped and thawed

Let's make our cinnamon sugar first by combining our sugar and cinnamon in a Mason jar, securing the lid, and giving it a good shake!

Pour canola oil into a Dutch oven until it's about ½ an inch deep. Heat that oil over medium-high heat until it's hot and shimmery. We're talking 400°F hot!

When the oil's ready to rock, carefully slide in 4 Uncrustables. Let 'em cook for about a minute until they're golden brown, then flip 'em and cook the other side. Keep an eye on 'em to make sure they don't burn. We want golden perfection here!

Using a spider strainer, scoop those fried beauties onto a plate lined with paper towels. Let 'em rest and let that excess oil drip away. Repeat the frying frenzy until you've cooked up all your Uncrustables.

Let 'em cool down. We're talking just slightly warm here. Sprinkle 'em with your cinnamon sugar and serve 'em up!

PIMM'S

MAKES 1 DRINK

HUSKY AND HANDSOME PIMM'S MARGARITA

WITH PUT ME ON EVERYTHING RUB

This is the margarita remix that you need! Ditch the ordinary Pimm's Cup and level up your summer soirées with this Husky and Handsome Pimm's Margarita. It's a flavor fiesta that combines the deep, aromatic magic of Pimm's with the tangy refreshment of tequila and lemon juice. And to really make this drink pop, we've got a secret weapon: a quick and easy AC Barbeque-inspired rim that gives it a distinct zip.

2 tablespoons Put Me on Everything Rub (page 203)

1 lemon wedge

1½ ounces tequila

¾ ounce Pimm's No. 1

¾ ounce lemon juice

Let's make this summer dream come true. Spread your Put Me on Everything Rub on a plate. Run a lemon wedge around the rim of your glass, then dip it into the barbeque rub magic. Set your glass aside.

Fill your cocktail shaker with ice, then add your tequila, Pimm's, and lemon juice. Shake it up well to get it nice and chilled. Strain the whole thing into the glass and prepare to be amazed! Ditch the ordinary and embrace the extraordinary.

MAKES 1 DRINK

CEDDY'S MICHELADA

Ditch the sugary sodas and boring beers! It's time to quench your thirst with a Ceddy's Michelada. This is a Mexican masterpiece that explodes with citrusy refreshment, savory depth, and a fiery kick straight outta St. Louis to keep things interesting.

2 tablespoons Old Vienna Red Hot Riplets Seasoning (or Old Bay if you prefer)

1 lime wedge

⅓ cup tomato juice (we prefer Spicy Hot V8)

Juice of ½ lime

2 shakes Worcestershire sauce

2 shakes soy sauce

2 shakes hot sauce

6 ounces Mexican lager beer

Spread your Red Hot Riplets Seasoning on a plate. Run a lime wedge around the rim of your pint glass, then dip it into that taste of St. Louis.

Fill your pint glass about halfway with ice cubes. Pour in your tomato juice and lime juice and shake in that Worcestershire sauce, soy sauce, and hot sauce. Give it a quick stir to combine all that goodness. Now for the star of the show: Slowly pour in your Mexican lager, letting it create a beautiful masterpiece. Garnish with your lime wedge and prepare to be amazed by this explosion of flavor.

Sol
CERVEZA

MAKES 6 DRINKS

DARK 'N' STORMY

Sunshine beating down? Burgers sizzling? Sounds like the perfect time to ditch the stress and embrace this Dark 'n' Stormy. Forget about fussy cocktails that require constant attention—this recipe's all about batching and relaxing.

We're talkin' a pitcher full of ginger beer bliss that lets you focus on what really matters: grill mastery, good conversation, and soaking up those summer vibes. This crowd-pleaser is easy to whip up and guaranteed to keep your guests cool, refreshed, and coming back for more. Grab your ingredients, crank up the tunes, and let the Dark 'n' Stormy be the MVP of your next cookout!

10 ounces dark rum
7 ounces lime juice, from 5 limes
5 ounces simple syrup
15 ounces ginger beer
2 limes, cut into wedges

In a pitcher, combine your dark rum, lime juice, and simple syrup. Give it a good stir to make sure everything's blended beautifully. Now for the real star: Top it all off with the ginger beer, letting it create a refreshing, bubbly masterpiece.

Set out that pitcher of deliciousness with a bowl of lime wedges for your guests to add at their leisure.

MAKES 6 DRINKS

HENNY COLADA

It's gettin' hot in these streets! That means one thing: time to chill out with a drink so good, it'll transport you straight to paradise. And we ain't talkin' no watered-down margarita. We're talkin' the Hennessy Colada. We're ditchin' the boring rum and switchin' things up with the smooth caramel goodness of Henny Cognac. It adds a layer of flavor so deep, it's like takin' a sip of the islands themselves.

1 (8.5-ounce) can cream of coconut

8 ounces pineapple juice

8 ounces Hennessy

Maraschino cherries (optional), for serving

Load your blender with 4 cups of ice, then throw in all that goodness: the cream of coconut, the pineapple juice, and the Hennessy. Blend it up smooth like a reggae beat.

Now, here's the important part: Pour that beautiful concoction into a big plastic container and shove it in the freezer for at least 2 hours. Patience is a virtue, especially when it comes to frozen drinks that are guaranteed to blow your mind. After it's all nice and frozen (or, should we say, "island-chilled"), take it out and give it a good stir. You want that creamy, dreamy consistency.

Grab your hurricane glasses if you're feelin' fancy. Pour it in and top it all off with a maraschino cherry on a stick for a garnish that's straight out of a beach postcard.

MAKES 6 DRINKS

SPIKED BRAZILIAN LEMONADE

Close your eyes and imagine this: sunshine on your face, toes in the sand, and a drink in your hand so good it'll make you forget all about those pesky deadlines. Well, open those eyes, because that dream drink is about to become your reality with this Spiked Brazilian Lemonade! And yes, this is a lemonade even though it's made with limes. In just five minutes, you can be sippin' on sunshine and forgetting about rent for a while (almost).

4 big limes, ends cut off, quartered

⅓ cup white sugar

7 ounces sweetened condensed milk

Coconut rum

In your blender, pulse the lime quarters, sugar, sweetened condensed milk, 4 cups cold water, and 4 cups ice until they are just combined. You're looking to extract flavor but not pulverize the limes.

Now, get your strainer ready. We gotta catch all that lime pulp; nobody wants that in their mini vacay. Pour the blended mixture over the strainer into a pitcher, leaving that pulp behind. Use a spoon to push out as much liquid as possible. Get rid of those rinds!

Grab a glass, fill it with ice, and pour in as much coconut rum as you would like (or omit it to make this nonalcoholic). Be careful, but a normal amount here would be about one shot's worth. Top it all off with your chilled Brazilian Lemonade and stir it up like a hurricane (without the mess, hopefully). Bonus points: Garnish that bad boy with a fun cocktail umbrella. Because who doesn't love a little extra island flair?

THE PANTRY

Let's dive deeper into the heart of BBQ country and explore the regional sauces and rubs that define the diverse and delicious world of American barbeque. Each region has its own unique flavors, techniques, and traditions that make it special, and we're here to celebrate them all.

Whether you're a fan of the tangy vinegar sauces of the Carolinas, the sweet and smoky sauces of the Midwest, or the bold and beefy flavors of Texas, this chapter is your ultimate guide to the regional sauces and rubs that define American barbeque. Get ready to explore, experiment, and enjoy the diverse and delicious world of BBQ flavors.

MAKES 2 CUPS

DR. CEDRIC'S BBQ SAUCE

Get ready to crank up the flavor with this legendary Dr. Cedric's BBQ sauce recipe. It's a mouthwatering melody of sweet, tangy, and smoky notes, guaranteed to elevate any backyard cookout.

1 (12-ounce) can Dr Pepper

½ cup ketchup

¼ cup molasses

2 tablespoons apple cider vinegar

1 tablespoon Worcestershire sauce

½ tablespoon Put Me on Everything Rub (page 203)

Now that you have all the ingredients assembled, it's time to create some BBQ magic! Simply combine the Dr Pepper, ketchup, molasses, vinegar, Worcestershire sauce, and rub in a saucepan and simmer over low heat until the sauce thickens to your desired consistency, about 30 minutes. Let it cool and store in an airtight container in your fridge. It's that easy!

MAKES 3/4 CUP

PUT ME ON EVERYTHING RUB

Hey, AC fam—lookin' to turn any dish into a flavor explosion? Then this Put Me on Everything Rub is your new best friend in your mouth (and on your grill). This is bold, smoky, finger-lickin'-good AC Barbeque magic in a jar.

6 tablespoons coarsely ground black pepper
2 tablespoons onion powder
2 tablespoons white sugar
4 teaspoons mustard powder
4 teaspoons garlic powder
2 teaspoons ancho powder
2 teaspoons Hungarian paprika

In a bowl, whisk together the pepper, onion powder, sugar, mustard powder, garlic powder, ancho powder, and paprika. This is your secret weapon for everything you can think of. Store in an airtight container in your cabinet for up to six months. We use it for so many recipes in this book, and you will too!

MAKES 2½ CUPS

SMOKY BEER BBQ SAUCE

We're about to turn you into a saucin' superhero with this Smoky Beer BBQ Sauce recipe. We're talkin' a symphony of flavors that'll have your taste buds doin' the two-step and your grill smokin' with envy. This sauce is the ultimate partner in crime for all your BBQ adventures. Whether you're slappin' ribs or smokin' some pulled pork, this bad boy will take your game to the next level.

1 (16-ounce) tall boy of your favorite light beer

1 (15-ounce) can tomato sauce

Juice of ½ lemon

½ cup apple cider vinegar

⅓ cup honey

¼ cup tomato paste

½ cup chopped yellow onion

¼ cup molasses

3 tablespoons Worcestershire sauce

2 tablespoons soy sauce

2 teaspoons liquid smoke

1 teaspoon smoked paprika

1 teaspoon garlic powder

½ teaspoon onion powder

½ teaspoon freshly ground black pepper

½ teaspoon kosher salt

½ teaspoon cayenne pepper

Grab a saucepan and add the beer, tomato sauce, lemon juice, vinegar, honey, tomato paste, onion, molasses, Worcestershire sauce, soy sauce, liquid smoke, paprika, garlic powder, onion powder, black pepper, salt, and cayenne pepper. Whisk all that deliciousness together like you're conducting a flavor orchestra. Crank up the heat to medium high and bring it to a simmer. Think of it as a gentle simmer, not a boil-over situation. Once it's simmering, reduce the heat to medium low and let it simmer uncovered for 20 minutes. We want that sauce to thicken up and get all nice and concentrated.

After 20 minutes, check out the consistency and pull it from the heat. Store in an airtight container in the fridge for up to 1 week.

MAKES 2 CUPS

GOLDEN MUSTARD BBQ SAUCE

Let's face it, Golden Mustard BBQ Sauce deserves a seat at the table beyond South Carolina. We love those classic Carolina twangs, but sometimes you gotta turn up the whole orchestra, you feel me? This is a flavor fiesta of sweet and heat for your pulled pork, your chops—heck, even your baked potato.

2 tablespoons vegetable oil

½ cup diced yellow onion

4 tablespoons finely minced red bell pepper

2 garlic cloves, minced

1 teaspoon freshly ground black pepper

1 teaspoon crushed red pepper flakes

1 teaspoon dried thyme

½ teaspoon celery salt

1 cup Dijon mustard

½ cup packed dark brown sugar

Juice of 1 lemon

¼ cup apple cider vinegar

3 tablespoons honey

2 teaspoons Worcestershire sauce

2 teaspoons tomato paste

1 teaspoon ground mustard

In a small saucepan, heat the oil over medium low. Add the onion and bell pepper and cook, stirring, until they're nice and soft, about 5 minutes. Add the garlic and cook, stirring, for another minute. Throw in the black pepper, red pepper flakes, thyme, and celery salt. Let them sizzle for a few minutes to release all that flavor.

Now comes the fun part! Add the mustard, brown sugar, lemon juice, vinegar, honey, Worcestershire sauce, tomato paste, and ground mustard and give it a good stir. Bring to a low boil for 3 minutes, then turn the heat down and simmer for 15 minutes, keepin' an eye on that mixture so it doesn't burn. Let your sauce cool slightly and then get ready to smother your favorite pork dish (or anything else your heart desires). Store in an airtight container in the fridge for up to 1 week.

MAKES 3 CUPS

ANCHO CHILE BBQ SAUCE

We're about to turn you into a BBQ legend with this Ancho Chile BBQ Sauce. This is magic in a bottle. We're talkin' smoky, sweet, and a little bit of heat—the perfect flavor trifecta to take your cookout from meh to Mamma Mia in minutes.

3 ancho chile peppers
½ yellow onion, diced
2 garlic cloves, crushed
1 cup packed dark brown sugar
½ cup tomato sauce
½ cup apple cider vinegar
3 tablespoons unsalted butter
2 tablespoons honey
1 tablespoon kosher salt
2 teaspoons freshly ground black pepper

First things first, we gotta wake up those ancho chiles. Bring 2 cups of water to a boil in a saucepan, then throw in those bad boys. Let them simmer for about 20 minutes, until they're nice and soft. We want them releasing all that smoky goodness! Then take them out and set that leftover liquid aside—we'll need it later.

Now, grab your blender and get ready to create some magic. Throw in those softened ancho chiles, along with the diced onion, garlic, and ½ cup of that leftover boiling liquid. Hit that pulse button until you have a smooth, beautiful sauce. Set it aside for now; we're almost there!

In your trusty skillet, combine the brown sugar, tomato sauce, vinegar, butter, honey, salt, and black pepper. Let it simmer for 10 minutes, low and slow, letting all those flavors get to know each other real well.

Once that sauce is lookin' all simmered and delicious, add that ancho chile mixture you whipped up in the blender. Stir it all together until it's nice and combined. Boom! You just made AC's Ancho Chile BBQ Sauce, the secret weapon of BBQ champions everywhere. Store in an airtight container in the fridge for up to 1 week.

BARBECUE

MAKES $^{2}/_{3}$ CUP

CARNE ASADA DRY RUB

We're talkin' a fiesta of Mexican spices that'll have your taste buds doin' the Macarena and your neighbors wonderin' what deliciousness you're cookin' up.

This rub is the secret weapon for grill masters who want their steak to be Husky and Handsome (and by that we mean juicy, flavorful, and smokin' hot). Just a sprinkle of this magic dust and your carne asada will be the star of the show, guaranteed.

3 tablespoons chili powder
2 tablespoons garlic powder
2 tablespoons onion powder
1 tablespoon Tajín seasoning
2 teaspoons ground cumin
2 teaspoons celery salt
2 teaspoons Mexican oregano
1 teaspoon ground coriander
Freshly ground black pepper

Grab a jar with a lid and throw in the chili powder, garlic powder, onion powder, Tajín, cumin, celery salt, oregano, coriander, and pepper like you're throwing a fiesta in a bowl. Shake it up like a Polaroid picture (or just shake it well) to get everything mixed nice and even.

Now, find a cool, dry spot to store that rub until you're ready to turn your next steak into a masterpiece. But remember, use a clean, dry spoon every time you grab some rub. We don't want any funky flavors messing up your fiesta.

St. Louis Dry
Rub, p. 213
Memphis Dry
Rub, p. 216
Put Me on
Everything
Rub, p. 203
Carne Asada
Dry Rub, p. 210

MAKES 2½ CUPS

ST. LOUIS BBQ SAUCE

Looking for a tangy, lip-smacking barbeque sauce that's perfect for ribs and more? Look no further than our St. Louis–style barbeque sauce! This sauce is a true St. Louis original, dating back to grocer Louis Maull in 1926. Unlike its Kansas City cousin, St. Louis–style barbeque sauce is thinner and a touch more tart, with a focus on grilling and saucing rather than slow cooking. It's simple to make with just a handful of ingredients, but it delivers on flavor in a big way.

While it's perfect for St. Louis–Style Ribs (page 46), this sauce can also be used on St. Louis Pork Steaks (page 54), beef steaks, or chicken, or even as a dipping sauce. Ready to get saucin'? Let's do it!

2 cups ketchup
⅓ cup apple cider vinegar
⅓ cup packed light brown sugar
2 tablespoons yellow mustard
1 tablespoon onion powder
1 tablespoon garlic powder
½ teaspoon cayenne pepper
¼ teaspoon kosher salt

Combine the ketchup, vinegar, brown sugar, mustard, onion powder, garlic powder, cayenne pepper, salt, and ½ cup water in a saucepan and cook over low heat. Let it simmer for 20 minutes, whisking occasionally. The sauce should be thin, but not watery. Remove the sauce from the heat and let it cool for 20 to 30 minutes. The sauce is good to use right away, but it's even better if you let it sit for a day in the fridge in an airtight container. This sauce can be stored in the refrigerator for up to a week or frozen for 3 months.

MAKES 2 CUPS

ST. LOUIS DRY RUB

There's one stop Cedric can't miss when he goes home to St. Louis: Pappy's Smokehouse. Their baby back ribs? Legendary. This is our ode to their dry rub that makes those baby back ribs sing. It's pretty darn close, and it'll keep your favorite BBQ enthusiast happy.

1 cup white sugar

½ cup packed light brown sugar

⅓ cup sea salt

2 tablespoons onion powder

2 tablespoons garlic powder

2 tablespoons paprika

3 tablespoons chili powder

2 tablespoons ancho chile powder

2 tablespoons cayenne pepper

2 tablespoons freshly ground black pepper

1 tablespoon crushed dried rosemary

2 tablespoons crushed dried thyme

2 tablespoons ground cumin

1 tablespoon ground nutmeg

1 tablespoon ground allspice

Grab a big bowl with a lid and toss in the white sugar, brown sugar, sea salt, onion powder, garlic powder, paprika, chili powder, ancho chile powder, cayenne pepper, black pepper, rosemary, thyme, cumin, nutmeg, and allspice. Shake it up well until everything's evenly mixed. Store this in your pantry for up to 6 months in an airtight container to keep the moisture out.

Ancho Chile BBQ Sauce, p. 207
St. Louis BBQ Sauce, p. 212
East Carolina Vinegar Sauce, p. 220
Dr. Cedric's BBQ Sauce, p. 202
Alabama White BBQ Sauce, p. 223
KC BBQ Sauce, p. 221

Memphis BBQ Sauce, p. 217
Lexington, North Carolina, BBQ Sauce, p. 219
Smoky Beer BBQ Sauce, p. 205
Texas Mop Sauce, p. 222
Golden Mustard BBQ Sauce, p. 206

MAKES 1½ CUPS

MEMPHIS DRY RUB

Take your grilling game to the next level with our dynamite Memphis Dry Rub. This rub isn't for the faint of heart! It captures the essence of Memphis-style barbeque with a perfect blend of smoky paprika, savory spices, and a kick of cayenne pepper.

¼ cup packed light brown sugar

¼ cup white sugar

¼ cup mild paprika

3 tablespoons kosher salt

1 tablespoon onion powder

1 tablespoon garlic powder

1 tablespoon cayenne pepper

1 tablespoon freshly ground black pepper

1 tablespoon chili powder

In a bowl, whisk together the brown sugar, white sugar, paprika, salt, onion powder, garlic powder, cayenne pepper, black pepper, and chili powder. This is your secret weapon for making Memphis-style barbeque at home! Store at room temperature in your favorite Mason jar—you know, the one that shines brighter than the others—for up to 6 months.

MAKES 3 CUPS

MEMPHIS BBQ SAUCE

Ditch the store-bought stuff—it's time to create your own legendary Memphis BBQ sauce right at home. This easy and delicious recipe is a guaranteed crowd-pleaser. It's versatile with a beautiful balance of sweetness, tang, and a touch of smokiness that complements anything you put it on.

2 cups ketchup

½ cup yellow mustard

½ cup packed light brown sugar

¼ cup apple cider vinegar

3 tablespoons Worcestershire sauce

2 tablespoons chili powder

1 tablespoon freshly ground black pepper

1 tablespoon onion powder

1 tablespoon garlic powder

2 teaspoons liquid smoke

2 teaspoons celery salt

½ teaspoon cayenne pepper

In a large saucepan, whisk together the ketchup, mustard, brown sugar, vinegar, Worcestershire sauce, chili powder, black pepper, onion powder, garlic powder, liquid smoke, celery salt, and cayenne pepper. Place the saucepan over medium heat and cook, stirring aggressively, until it starts to boil. The sauce is thick and can burn easily. Remove it from the heat occasionally and stir well.

Once the sauce is boiling, reduce the heat to low, cover the pan, and simmer for 30 minutes. Just be sure to stir occasionally to prevent sticking. Store leftover sauce in the refrigerator for 5 days. For longer storage, freeze it in small portions for up to 3 months.

THE

MAKES 2 CUPS

LEXINGTON, NORTH CAROLINA, BBQ SAUCE

Buckle up for a trip to Lexington, North Carolina, the land of legendary vinegar-based barbeque. This recipe will guide you through crafting the authentic Lexington-style dip BBQ sauce, a true taste of Southern tradition. In North Carolina, this recipe can be made with white or apple cider vinegar. We prefer apple cider because it has more tang, but you can easily sub in white. We use a generous amount of vinegar for a bold, lip-smacking flavor that cuts through rich barbeque like a champ. And a hint of ketchup and apple juice balances the tang with a touch of sweetness, creating a perfect flavor harmony. This sauce is the ultimate champion of the mop basting style.

1 cup apple cider vinegar (or white vinegar)

¼ cup ketchup

¼ cup apple juice

3 tablespoons packed light brown sugar

½ tablespoon kosher salt

1 teaspoon hot sauce

1 teaspoon crushed red pepper flakes

1 teaspoon finely ground black pepper

In a bowl, whisk together the vinegar, ketchup, apple juice, brown sugar, salt, hot sauce, red pepper flakes, and black pepper until everything is beautifully combined. Now comes the important part—letting the flavors meld. Cover the bowl and refrigerate your sauce for at least 3 hours. Overnight is even better.

Once your sauce has reached peak flavor potential, divide it in two. Use one half for basting your barbeque during cooking, applying it with a silicone brush for easy cleaning. The other half goes into a squeeze bottle for your guests to drizzle on their barbeque creations at the table.

There you have it, folks! With this recipe, you can bring the legendary taste of Lexington-style barbeque to your own backyard.

MAKES $1\frac{3}{4}$ CUPS

EAST CAROLINA VINEGAR SAUCE

East Carolina BBQ is all about balancing the richness of slow-cooked pork with a vibrant, acidic punch. That's where the vinegar comes in! Our recipe uses distilled vinegar for a clean, tangy flavor that cuts through the fat and keeps your taste buds happy. This sauce is a testament to the "less is more" philosophy. Just a few key ingredients come together to create a flavor that's both bold and sophisticated. This versatile sauce does double duty. Use it as a mop to baste your meat while it cooks, infusing it with flavor and keeping it moist. The same sauce can also be served on the side for dipping or drizzling.

$1\frac{1}{2}$ cups white vinegar

1 teaspoon hot sauce

2 tablespoons white sugar

1 tablespoon kosher salt

2 teaspoons crushed red pepper flakes

2 teaspoons finely ground black pepper

In a jar, combine the vinegar, hot sauce, sugar, salt, red pepper flakes, and black pepper and give them a good shake to make sure everything is well acquainted. Let your sauce sit for at least 12 hours to allow the flavors to meld and mature. The longer you wait, the deeper and more complex the flavor will become. When it's time to cook, pour a small amount of sauce into a separate cup for mopping. Baste your meat with the sauce every hour or so during the cooking process.

LOCAL TIP: East Carolina barbeque is traditionally served with a whole hog as the star of the show. However, this delicious sauce goes perfectly with any cut of slow-cooked pork.

MAKES 5 CUPS

KC BBQ SAUCE

We all know that store-bought stuff just doesn't cut it. You gotta have a secret weapon in your fridge, a sauce so good your guests will be begging for the recipe. This is a Husky and Handsome tribute to the bold, smoky flavors that put Kansas City barbeque on the map.

Forget about mystery ingredients and questionable additives. This sauce is all-natural, all-delicious, and all-perfect for smothering your next cookout masterpiece. We're talkin' layers on layers of flavor: sweet, tangy, smoky, with a kick that'll have your taste buds doin' a two-step.

2 tablespoons chili powder

2 teaspoons kosher salt

1 teaspoon freshly ground black pepper

2 cups ketchup

1 cup packed dark brown sugar

½ cup honey

½ cup apple cider vinegar

½ cup yellow mustard

⅓ cup Worcestershire sauce

¼ cup dark molasses

1 teaspoon hot sauce

Vegetable oil

1 yellow onion, chopped

4 garlic cloves, minced

In a small bowl, combine the chili powder, salt, and pepper. In a large separate bowl, mix together that wet posse: ketchup, brown sugar, honey, vinegar, mustard, Worcestershire sauce, molasses, and hot sauce. Now you are ready to get down.

Heat up enough oil to just coat the bottom of a large saucepan. Add the onion and cook, stirring, until softened, about 5 minutes. Then add the garlic and cook, stirring, for another minute. Add the small bowl of dry spice mix and stir it in for 2 minutes to get those spices fragrant. Pour in the wet ingredients and simmer for 15 minutes with the lid off, lettin' that sauce thicken up nicely. This sauce is your ticket to becoming a backyard BBQ legend. Get cookin' and turn any cookout into a championship-worthy event. Store in an airtight container in the fridge for up to 1 week.

MAKES 5 CUPS

TEXAS MOP SAUCE

Ditch the ketchup and sugar bombs, 'cause we're goin' on a Texas-sized flavor adventure with this authentic Texas Mop Sauce. This ain't no thick, gloppy mess. We're talkin' a thin, spicy symphony that penetrates deep into your meat, infusing every bite with smoky goodness.

1 tablespoon unsalted butter

1 yellow onion, finely chopped

1 tablespoon mild paprika

2 teaspoons freshly ground black pepper

2 teaspoons chili powder

1 teaspoon ground cumin

1 green bell pepper, seeded and chopped (about 2 cups)

4 garlic cloves, minced

2 cups beef broth

1 cup Lone Star beer (or any other lager)

¼ cup ketchup

¼ cup apple cider vinegar

3 tablespoons Worcestershire sauce

3 tablespoons steak sauce

2 tablespoons packed light brown sugar

2 teaspoons hot sauce

In a small saucepan, melt your butter and sweat those onions, stirring, until they're translucent, about 5 minutes.

While the onions are cooking down, mix together your paprika, pepper, chili powder, and cumin in a small bowl. Set aside.

When your onions are done, add the bell pepper, garlic, and your spice mix. Let it sizzle for a couple of minutes to release all those delicious flavors. Add the beef broth, beer, ketchup, vinegar, Worcestershire sauce, steak sauce, brown sugar, and hot sauce and whisk until well blended. Give it a good stir and let it simmer for 15 minutes.

Taste test and adjust the seasonings to your liking. There you have it: Lone Star liquid gold! This sauce is the secret weapon that'll make your next cookout a legendary Texas-style BBQ experience. Store in an airtight container in the fridge for up to 1 week.

MAKES 4 CUPS

ALABAMA WHITE BBQ SAUCE

We're ditchin' the ordinary and headin' to flavortown with this Alabama White BBQ Sauce. This is a creamy, tangy dreamboat that'll add an unexpected and unforgettable zip to your next smoked chicken cookout.

1½ cups mayonnaise

½ cup apple cider vinegar

Juice of 2 lemons

½ cup apple juice

2 tablespoons white sugar

2 tablespoons prepared horseradish

2 tablespoons freshly ground black pepper

2 teaspoons mustard powder

1 teaspoon kosher salt

½ teaspoon cayenne pepper

Throw that mayonnaise, vinegar, lemon juice, apple juice, sugar, horseradish, black pepper, mustard powder, salt, and cayenne pepper in a big bowl and whisk it together until it's smooth and creamy. Cover it up and stick it in the fridge for at least 2 hours (longer is even better) to let all those flavors meld together into a symphony of deliciousness. Store in an airtight container in the fridge for up to 1 week.

ACKNOWLEDGMENTS

**IRST AND FOREMOST,** thank you to everyone who helped turn this idea into something real. From a shared love of barbeque and family to a restaurant, a product line, our television show *Kings of BBQ*, and now a cookbook, it's been an incredible journey.

Big love to our AC fam: To Burt Bachman, our pitmaster; this wouldn't be what it is without you. To Rasheed Phillips, Adam Perry Lang, Kevin Bludso, Joey Victorian, Chef Jeff, Chuck "Flavor Train," Chef Ked, Paula "Queen of the Grill" Stachyra, Big Moe, and the many chefs and BBQ lovers who've supported our rubs and sauces across social media, thank you; we see you, and we appreciate you.

To our incredible team at AC Barbeque, thank you for believing in the vision and bringing the flavor every single day: Ben Silverman, Drew Buckley, Eric Rhone, Brian Dobbins, Robert Earl, and the rest of the crew who helped guide this brand from the ground up. Thank you to David Grieve for the advice.

And a special shout-out to Linh Le (The Rock) and Diego Tapia (The Swiss Army Knife) for always showing up with answers, ideas, and love.

To our publishing team: Thank you to Ian Kleinert, Garrett McGrath, Emily Carr, Joshua Jasper, Matt Sayles, Ed Rudolph, Anna Lee, Leanna Rongavilla, and Alicia Buszczak for helping us bring this book to life with care and creativity. Also thank you to Justin Schwartz, Gina Navaroli, and everyone at Simon & Schuster and Simon Element; we couldn't have done this without you.

This cookbook is more than recipes. It's a celebration of where we come from, the people who fed us, and the tables we've gathered around. Thank you for joining us.

—Anthony & Cedric

I'd like to acknowledge my grandfather, uncles, aunts, and mom, but in particular my father, Sterling Bowman, for teaching me the ways of a true pitmaster. He showed me how barbecuing is about more than just food—it's about family and community. For that, I thank you, Dad, and dedicate this cookbook to you. I love you and miss you!

—Anthony

First, let me shout out my grandmother Mrs. Rosie Boyce. It was those first home-cooked meals surrounded by family and loved ones that set the tone for what dinner and gatherings should strive to be.

To my beloved mother, thank you for keeping that joyful atmosphere of food and family alive throughout my life.

"For Days!" That was my uncle Lloyd's catchphrase. He could make it apply to anything—especially when he was on the grill, cooking ribs, chops, links, and his famous pig snout, all while DJing the party. I can still hear the Intruders' "Cowboys to Girls" and smell that barbeque. This book is a culinary road trip back to that feeling, and we hope it brings you there too.

Big shout-out to my wife, Lorna Kyles. You're all the inspiration I need.

—Cedric

INDEX

C

S

T

Discover the Spirit
GGZ 189
NORTH DAKOTA
Kentucky
879 LBG
KENTON
MAINE
568899
Vacationland
RAILWAY
ENJOY
Royal Crown

An Imprint of Simon & Schuster, LLC
1230 Avenue of the Americas
New York, NY 10020

First Simon Element hardcover edition May 2026

Interior design by Janet Evans-Scanlon

Manufactured in China

10 9 8 7 6 5 4 3 2 1

Library of Congress Cataloging-in-Publication Data has been applied for.

ISBN 978-1-6680-7535-7
ISBN 978-1-6680-7536-4 (ebook)